# THE
# STRIPED
# BASS
# CHRONICLES

# Books by George Reiger

*Zane Grey: Outdoorsman*

*Profiles in Saltwater Angling*

*Fishing with McClane*

*The Zane Grey Cookbook* (co-authored with Barbara Reiger)

*The Audubon Society Book of Marine Wildlife*

*The Wings of Dawn*

*The Undiscovered Zane Grey Fishing Stories*

*Wanderer on My Native Shore*

*Southeast Coast*

*Floaters and Stick-Ups*

*The Birder's Journal*

*The Wildfowler's Quest*

*The Silver King*

*The Bonefish*

*Heron Hill Chronicle*

*The Striped Bass Chronicles*

# THE
# STRIPED
# BASS
# CHRONICLES

*The Saga of America's Great Game Fish*

by
## George Reiger

*Illustrated by Christopher Reiger*

LYONS & BURFORD, PUBLISHERS

Printed in the United States of America

10  9  8  7  6  5  4  3  2  1

Design by Jennifer Corsano


Library of Congress Cataloging-in-Publication Data

Reiger, George, 1939–
    The striped bass chronicles: the saga of America's great game
fish / by George Reiger; illustrated by Christopher Reiger.
        p.    cm.
    Includes bibliographical references and index.
    ISBN 1-55821-478-X
    1. Striped bass fishing.   2. Striped bass.   I. Title.
SH691.S7R45   1997
799.1'7732'0973—dc21                                        97-1925
                                                              CIP

FOR DAD, who steered me in the right direction—
FOR MOM, who never understood, nor approved,
but finally let me be what I became—
And for my son and favorite fishing companion,
CHRISTOPHER,
who somehow found time during
his freshman year at the College of William and Mary
to illustrate this book.

# Contents

# Acknowledgments

I'd like to thank bookseller Ken Callahan, who has a better angling and natural history file in his head than most libraries have in their computers; Bill Feinberg and Dave Preble, who supplied me with old club records from, respectively, the Jersey Shore and Cuttyhunk Island; *publisher* Nick Lyons, who encouraged me to run this race by providing me with the starting blocks of a contract and advance, and *editor* Nick Lyons, for demanding more from me than I initially gave; and James H. Phillips, for serving as my intellectual pace-setter. So many ideas spiral up between us, it's often difficult to separate his contributions from mine. Finally, I need to thank my wife, Barbara, who—despite her long and often exhausting days at the Eastern Shore Public Library—got up at dawn each day to word-process what this computer-illiterate had written during the night.

# Introduction

The striped bass has played such an important role in my life, it's time I repaid the debt with a book about the fish and its effect on thousands of other people. First, however, a little about the striper and me.

Although my dad was one of the smartest and most disciplined men I've ever known—a practicing physician by an age (twenty-one) when most pre-meds are still finishing college—he was too competitive and self-absorbed to be compassionate, even with his sons. When he took my older brother and me on big-game fishing trips to Nova Scotia and the Bahamas, he did the fishing. Only if we stayed out of the way while he fought the marlin and giant tuna would he allow us to fish with handlines for mangrove snapper off the dock at Bimini, or for cod when the tide slackened in Soldier's Rip.

Striped bass interested my father, but only the biggest specimens. A forty-plus-pound striper is fifteen or more years old. Such fish are always scarce and were so even in New York coastal waters in the early 1950s. Nonetheless, Dad was determined to catch the largest striper by a member of the Lawrence (Long Island) Yacht Club.

To catch a big striper, you have to fish at night. And to fish safely at night from a boat close to the beach, Dad needed extra eyes and hands. Since by this time my older brother would no longer fish with him, Dad needed me.

I've never shared my father's obsession with trophy fish. Being able to hook fish consistently—especially when other anglers claim there're none around or they're not biting—provides my angling highs. Still, I felt an exhilaration mingled with dread whenever Dad and I left the house for a night of striped bass trolling. A rush of adrenaline came when the boat rose over the first unseen swells of the Atlantic, and came again whenever breaking waves loomed unexpectedly out of the star-studded darkness.

Red lights were supposed to mark the ends of jetties, but the lights didn't always work. One black night, a surf fisherman warned us away from a jetty with a pyramid sinker that shattered the port windshield—fortunately, not the one I was peering through trying to see the light.

That smashed windshield wasn't the only wound inflicted on Dad's boat by shore fishermen. Over time, she acquired several scars on her wood hull, cabin roof, and cockpit deck where irate anglers had slung lead to keep us offshore. Dad hurled curses back, and I had a right to be equally angry about the criminal response to our unintentional violation of the shore fishermen's casting zones. Yet I usually felt more guilt than anger. I reasoned that Dad and I had the greater mobility to fish elsewhere. Moreover, there was my growing sense that a shore-fought striper is superior game—regardless of its size—to one taken from a boat. The jetty-jockeys held the sporting high ground because they fought striped bass from the rocks rather than merely dredging them up by trolling.

By the early 1960s, I'd abandoned several more conventional careers to try my hand at freelance writing. I lived in a one-room apartment over a garage in Berkeley, California, where my principal recreation was headboat fishing for striped bass. I preferred stripers to the more glamorous chinook and coho salmon, because stripers, like me, were easterners learning to cope in an exotic setting. Later, between tours in Vietnam—when I taught at the U.S. Naval Academy—Chesapeake stripers provided me with the continuity I craved amid the culture shock of coming home to a country where I'd become a stranger.

The striped bass is a wonderfully adaptable species that has evolved into a number of stocks distinguished by fin-ray and lateral-line scale counts. These stocks include fish from: the Bay of Fundy; the Hudson, with genetic distinctions between stripers living up-river and those in the estuary that disperse during the summer through the New York Bight, Long Island Sound, and as far north as Maine, and from which Pacific stripers are also descended; Chesa-peake tributaries, including spawning fish that spend their summers in New England and even Nova Scotia; the Roanoke River and sounds of North Carolina; the Santee-Cooper drainage in South Car-olina, with an evolving difference between the freshwater (land-locked) and coastal populations; the St. Johns River in Florida; and the Gulf of Mexico, with one stock (possibly two), found from west-ern Florida to Louisiana and up the Mississippi as far as Vicksburg.

Besides their capacity to move freely between rivers and the sea, striped bass find food at every level of the water column—slow, bot-tom-dwelling invertebrates as well as swift prey at the surface. And unlike salmon, which must spawn in their natal streams, striped bass will use any appropriate alternative to satisfy their procreative im-pulse. When, for example, the Conowingo Dam blocked access to the Susquehanna River—formerly the most important striped bass spawning tributary in the Chesapeake watershed—spawning stripers turned into the Chesapeake and Delaware Canal; there, sufficient current keeps the stripers' neutrally buoyant eggs from settling to the bottom and possibly smothering in silt, and from rising to the surface, where they could be contaminated by industrial residues.

The striper's resilience, fecundity, wide distribution, and potentially long life have made the species a major piscatorial player throughout our nation's history. And what is our history but the story of people impacting nature and nature impacting them? Our forebears (Amerindians, Inuits and Asians from the East, and Europeans and Africans from the West) absorbed and were absorbed by the bounty of a pristine continent and the cornucopian qualities of its coastal waters. Such abundance shaped values that the rest of the world has come to regard as uniquely American, and provided our ancestors with the means to fashion a future that's now our past.

Marcel Proust once observed that the only true paradises are those we've lost. The striper's many attributes give us the possibility of proving that one of those paradises can be regained—but only if we have the will to manage the fish for optimum yield rather than continuing the morally and scientifically bankrupt rationales of maximum exploitation.

## · 1 ·

# EARLY RECORDS

H AD OUR FOUNDING fathers chosen a fish rather than a bird as our national emblem, it would have had to have been the striped bass. The cod was important in New England but found in no great abundance south of Delaware. By contrast, the striped bass fed English colonists from Maine to Georgia. And although shad and herring once ran almost every river up and down the Atlantic Coast, their abundance lasted only a few weeks a year, while the striper was present for months at a time in the North, and year-round in the South.

Few early accounts of colonial fisheries don't include at least one reference to the quality and abundance of striped bass. In 1623, the settlers at Plymouth sustained themselves through the summer on stripers caught with just one net, fished from a single boat. In 1631, Captain John Smith noted that "there hath beene taken a thousand Basses at a draught." In 1635, William Wood suggested lobsters as bait for stripers. In 1639, the general court of the Massachusetts Bay Colony forbade its two most valuable resources—cod and striped bass—from being used for fertilizer.

In Force's early-seventeenth-century *Historical Tracts,* we find the following: "There is a Fish called a Basse. . . . Of this Fish our Fishers take many hundreds together, which I have seene lying on the shore to my admiration; yea, *their Nets ordinarily take more than they are able to haul to Land,* & for want of Boats & Men they are constrained to let many go after they have taken them, & yet sometimes they fill two Boats at a time with them."

In 1675, Sir John Josselyn (or Jocelyn) noted in his *Voyages* that "the Basse is a salt-water fish too, but most [are] taken in Rivers where they spawn; there hath been 3,000 *Basse* taken at a set." He reported that they traveled in vast schools and lashed the surface to foam in pursuit of forage fish. He called them savage predators that fought and tore the nets of fishermen. In 1670, the striper's abundance even helped found the first public schools in Plymouth through an excise tax on any sale of the fish.

The striped bass's tolerance of all salinity levels, from open ocean to pure fresh water, enables it to adapt to rivers and reservoirs far from the sea. In the first decade of this century, western writer Zane Grey caught striped bass while angling for black bass near his home at the confluence of Lackawaxen Creek and the Delaware River, some two hundred miles upstream from Philadelphia. The fish negotiated locks to take up residence in New York's Mohawk River, and striped bass may once have traveled up the St. Lawrence River as far as Lake Ontario, where fashion editor Genio C. Scott said he caught them prior to the American Civil War.

In 1879 and again in 1882, the striped bass went west with the pioneers when several hundred, mostly fingerlings, were transplanted from a New Jersey river via train, wagon, and wooden bucket to the upper estuary of San Francisco Bay. Some accounts say one or both California stockings came from the Navesink River; others say from the Shrewsbury River. Since the Navesink (flowing west to east) and the Shrewsbury (flowing south to north) ebb together into Raritan Bay behind Sandy Hook, they comprise the same tidal ecosystem. Thus, all Pacific stripers are descended from the same Hudson River gene pool. Like the settlers who'd preceded them, the Atlantic coastal fish flourished in their new surroundings, and within a few decades were found from central California to central Oregon.

When the first English settlers arrived in Massachusetts, they assumed that creatures they saw on this side of the Atlantic were much the same as those they'd known at home. The osprey, for example, has the same habit of hovering, then folding its wings and plunging down to feed, as the European buzzard—even though the osprey plunges into water, while the buzzard plunges onto land. Nonetheless, the colonists saw the similarity in behavior and named "Buzzards Bay" after the many ospreys, or "fish buzzards," feeding and nesting along its shores. A generation later, other colonists linked the soaring habits of the buzzard and the naked head and neck of the wild turkey to come up with another American "buzzard"—the turkey buzzard, or turkey vulture.

The colonists made similar associations with the different fish they called "bass." Although the saltwater European bass lacks stripes, it and the American striped bass are not only alike in overall form, but they also share many of the same habits. As the modern *Collins Guide to the Sea Fishes of Britain and North-Western Europe* notes, the bass is "a very voracious predatory fish, which usually lives in small shoals close to rocky coasts and in large estuaries."

There are, however, some significant differences. The European bass reproduces at sea, while the striped bass spawns in the intertidal zone or fall line of large coastal rivers. A European bass is huge at fifteen pounds, while the striped bass has been recorded at over one hundred pounds. We know today, however, that all large specimens of both bass are female. For example, almost every striper of over thirty pounds is a "cow," and not a "bull," as old-timers were wont to call big fish. Since everything from oysters to evergreens grew larger in the New World, it was natural for the first colonists familiar with both fish to assume a connection, although it took scientists another two hundred years to confirm it.

As recently as 1966, taxonomists were still wrestling over the striper's scientific nomenclature. That year, P. J. P. Whitehead and A. C. Wheeler removed the striped bass from the genus *Roccus*—where it had been for decades—and returned it to *Morone*. This was because naturalist Samuel Latham Mitchill (1764–1831) initially assigned the striped bass to the genus *Morone,* then decided it was more suitable in the genus *Roccus,* and finally settled on *Perca.* However, under the rules of scientific naming adopted after Mitchill's death, a name can never be changed, even by the person who created it. So the striped bass, along with three other American fish long assigned to the genus *Roccus*—white perch, white bass, and yellow bass—were reassigned to *Morone.* Simultaneously, W. A. Gosline founded a new sub-family, Percichthyidae, within the Serranidae (basslike fish) and moved the striped bass and its three American relatives into it.

The situation was even more confusing a generation ago. In 1937, ichthyologist Daniel Merriman used *Roccus lineatus* as the striper's scientific name in a definitive study of the species. Four years later, he used *Roccus saxatilis* in an even more definitive study completed for the U.S. Fish and Wildlife Service. Since this seventy-seven-page federal bulletin was *the* scientific account of the striped bass for its time, and since *Roccus* is a more spirited name than *Morone,* some older anglers would still rather fight than switch.

Two years after Mitchill's death, a medical doctor named Jerome Van Crowninshield Smith mocked Mitchill for the name he'd preferred: *Perca mitchilli.* Writing in his *Natural History of the Fishes of Massachusetts* (1833), Dr. Smith noted that Mitchill "might with equal propriety have tacked his name to the white shark, or the bones of the mastodon, and the last would have savored less of vanity, than the affixing his cognomen to a common table fish, known from time immemorial, all over Europe."

A decade later, New York tackle dealer John J. Brown added his two cents' worth. Writing in *The American Angler's Guide* (1845), Brown stated that "if the above assertion of Smith's is correct, it is very strange that so important [a game]fish has not been known to the angling community of Europe; for out of upwards of an hundred books on the subject of angling, in Europe, only one or two makes mention of any kind of basse whatever, and they are a species of trout, differing entirely from the striped basse of our waters."

The reason European angling writers made little mention of their native bass was that most of them were—well, frankly—*snobs* who considered trout and salmon to be the only true gamefish. Saltwater species were best left to fishmongers. Only toward the latter half of the nineteenth century, and then only following the example of more egalitarian American writers, did a few British anglers begin acknowledging there was good sport to be had in the sea. At last, in 1895, the distinguished Badminton Library series of outdoor books published in London devoted an entire volume to *Sea Fishing*, including a chapter on fly fishing and featuring several pages on the techniques and pleasure of casting to European bass.

Although Dr. Smith may have been envious, and John J. Brown merely ignorant, such early observers' confusion over the relationship between European bass and American striped bass was largely semantic. Dr. Smith quoted "the late distinguished De Witt Clinton"[1] to the effect that *bass* is a Dutch word "signifying *perch*." In colonial days, "bass" and "perch" were used interchangeably on both sides of the Atlantic to describe a spectrum of not always closely related fishes. That's why it's ironically appropriate that *perch* was the root of W. A. Gosline's new family name for the striped bass: Percichthyidae.

We don't, however, read the early angling writers for their scientific expertise; we read them for their anecdotes of a bygone age. When Dr. Smith got down to reporting what he knew, he had some wonderful things to tell us about the striper's role in early-nineteenth-century American life: "Striped basse are a sea fish, but principally subsist near the mouths of rivers, up which they run as high as they can conveniently go. During the approach of winter, instead of striking out into the deep water of the open ocean, like most other anadromous species, the basse finds a residence in ponds, coves, rivers and still arms of the sea, where, undisturbed and comfortable it remains till the following spring. The principal rivers in the state of Maine, as the Penobscot, &c., are the places where they are now taken in the greatest abundance, and of the finest flavor and size."

---

[1]"Clinton" is the family name of the earls of Lincoln and the dukes of Newcastle. One of the ironies of the Revolutionary War is that De Witt Clinton's father, James, and his uncle, George, were both brigadier generals on the American side while their distant cousin, Sir Henry Clinton, was commander in chief—until his quarrel with Charles Cornwallis and subsequent resignation in 1781—of the British army. In time, De Witt Clinton became mayor of New York City, governor of the state, and, in 1812, the Peace Party candidate in the presidential election won by Madison.

In 1944, Oliver Hazard Perry Rodman noted in his book on the *Striped Bass* that in "the good old days, according to Boston's Dana Chapman, experienced tackle merchant and angler in his own right, when, if the fishing in the spring got a little slow in the famed [Penobscot] Bangor Pool (Maine) for salmon, the boys used to bend on a red and white bucktail fly that was tied fairly full and take themselves a mess of striped bass. These flies had a joint about half an inch back from the eye so that the hook was free to swing—not such a bad idea, either."

Today, the Kennebec is the most important striped bass river in Maine. This is partly because it has too many dams ever to redeem itself as a salmon river. It's also because, historically, the first Atlantic salmon caught in the Penobscot each year was sent to the White House. Fishery restoration efforts in the Penobscot have consequently concentrated on Atlantic salmon, while those in the Kennebec have focused on striped bass.

Meanwhile, Dr. Smith had this delightful anecdote of stripers past: "A striped basse, weighing forty pounds, was taken by a colored servant on the banks of Harlaem river [New York], a little south of the bridge. The fish was discovered by the man from the end of the dock, which projected some distance into the river. At times he [the fish, not the man] would sail gently along past the dock into quite shoal water, but how to capture him was the question. No net, or hook and bait was at hand, and as the golden opportunity might not last long, our hero resolved to encounter him single handed in his native element, and at a favorable moment he leaped from the dock directly upon his back. The affrighted fish darted from under him as though a shark was in pursuit, and as luck would have it, took a direction for the shore, and ran up nearly high and dry into the mud. Before he could get fairly afloat again, and have plenty of sea room to make his escape, the colored man seized him by the gills, dragged him upon the beach, and secured his prize."

Dr. Smith is a secondary source of the oft-repeated tale of how, in 1670, the court at Plymouth Colony created the New World's first public school through the sale of fish. His information was based on a paragraph in Deane's *History of Scituate* reporting that all profits from the mackerel, herring, and striped bass fisheries (but not those for cod or haddock) went to support the free school in Plymouth. In 1677, these revenues were distributed among several other schools on Cape Cod. In 1692, after the union of all the Massachusetts outposts into one colony, other public funds were used for the schools.

Dr. Smith was remarkably prescient for someone writing over 160 years ago. He predicted that "when the population of the country is about ten times its present amount [the population of the United States is now more than twenty times greater than it was in Smith's day], a vast number of animals, now discarded from the catalogue of edibles, will necessarily be considered in the light of luxuries and indispensable necessaries."

He believed that so-called trash species such as skate and dogfish would one day replace such delectable, but soon-to-be-diminished, fish as striped bass. Today, skate and dogfish are indeed marketable, whereas only a generation ago, they were quite literally worthless. The human population of the United States continues to escalate at twenty-five to thirty million people per decade, and even a common marine snail such as the whelk now brings a pretty penny when it's marketed as "conch." Yet, remarkably, the striped bass continues to hold its own as an important commercial species. This has been done, however, at a cost to recreational fishermen, who usually find their sport with whatever is left after the netters are through.

# · 2 ·

# OUR FLY-FISHING PIONEER

WE'LL NEVER KNOW who caught the first striped bass on a fly. Undoubtedly someone did, even before the 1810s, when statesman Daniel Webster took his first streamer-caught striper from the Potomac River. Yet it wasn't until the 1840s that an exiled aristocrat and remittance man named Henry William Herbert recommended fly fishing for striped bass as a regular pastime. More important, Herbert—writing under the pen name "Frank Forester"—introduced the patrician concept of sportsmanship to democratic America. He was the first writer to compare striped bass with Atlantic salmon—a comparison that has both helped and hobbled the striper's reputation to the present. The comparison lifted the striper into its nineteenth-century niche as salt water's premier gamefish, especially when caught on a fly. At the same time, however, the striper has never quite escaped the longer shadow cast by the more prestigious salmon.

Two lawyers, Philo T. Ruggles and Anson Livingston, supervised the modest trust that Herbert's father established for his son in America. Ruggles and Livingston were so discreet that biographers still have little idea why the twenty-four-year-old Herbert was forced to flee England in 1831 and spend the remainder of his foreshortened life—he committed suicide in 1858—in the United States. Herbert spent his early years in America living in a small apartment in lower Manhattan near the school where he taught Latin and Greek, and supplemented his modest income by freelance writing. Ruggles and Livingston asked Herbert's father to provide the young man with a more substantive residence, especially after his American wife died and left him with a son. As an alien, Herbert's father couldn't own property in New York State, so Ruggles and Livingston bought in his name an acre and a quarter overlooking New Jersey's Passaic River, just a short row upstream from the burgeoning town of Newark. Herbert frequently fly fished for striped bass in front of the house he built there in 1845.

Herbert was fortunate in his trustees, for not only were Ruggles and Livingston genuinely concerned with his welfare, but they also shared his enthusiasm for angling. Ruggles, in particular, was a passionate fly fisherman. He felt, however, that fly tackle was inappropriate for salt water; the marine environment was simply too harsh and coarse for the refined likes of fly tackle and fly fishermen. By contrast, Herbert's servant, Charlie Holt, enthusiastically endorsed his master's use of a fly rod to catch herring, shad, mackerel, and—especially—striped bass on the flies that Charlie tied.

If Herbert's tastes were selective, his interests were ecumenical, and he eventually tried almost every form of gear for almost every fish found in the New York Bight. In *Frank Forester's Fish and Fishing* (1849), he concluded that "those fish which never visit salt water are unquestionably so much inferior to others of their own family which run periodically to the sea, that they are with great difficulty recognized as belonging to the same order with their roving brethren while of those, none of which are known to leave the fresh water, but two or three kinds, are worth taking at all; and even these are not to be compared with the migratory, or the pure sea fish."

Although he preferred fly fishing, Herbert accepted the fact that for some species and in some circumstances, a fly rod is inappropriate. That's why he suggested that, although preparing a squid bait for striped bass may not be as aesthetic as tying a streamer, it's essential if you want to hook the "very large fish" that show little interest in "Salmon flies." Regardless of how you fish for stripers, however, "with the sole exception of Salmon fishing, [striped bass offer] the finest of the seaboard varieties of piscatorial sport. The Striped Bass is the boldest, bravest, strongest, and most active fish that visits the waters of the Midland States, and is, as I have before observed, to be surpassed only by the Salmon."

Although written for the all-around angler, *Frank Forester's Fish and Fishing* advocated fly fishing throughout.

Herbert noted that "the fly will take [stripers] brilliantly, and at the end of three hundred yards of Salmon-line a twelve-pound Bass will be found quite sufficient to keep even the most skilful [sic] angler's hands as full as he can possibly desire."

Fifteen years later, Thaddeus Norris mocked Herbert in *The American Angler's Book* (1864) by observing that "the author in question must have delighted in 'magnificent distances;' for a line of three hundred yards, with a Bass at the end of it, would certainly be 'playing at long taw,' and is suggestive of 'shooting with a long bow.' Most anglers will kill a Bass of any size, and not give him fifty yards of line." (Norris, however, must never have hooked a large striper in a strong current.)

Herbert wasn't selective about the flies he used. "The larger and gaudier, the better," he wrote. "None is more taking than an orange body with peacock and blue jay wings and black hackle legs; but any of the well-known Salmon flies will secure him as will the scarlet-bodied fly with scarlet ibis and silver pheasant wings, which is so killing to the Black Bass of the lakes."

It baffled Herbert that fly fishing for smallmouth and large-mouth bass was becoming popular while fly fishing for striped bass was still largely unknown. "It is singular," he wrote, "that more recourse is not had to this mode of taking him, as in waters where the Salmon is not, there is no sport equal to it. Those who try this method will not, I dare to assert, regret the trial."

Herbert did, however, put his finger on the one drawback of striper fly fishing: Anglers "must fish from a boat, as the width of the streams which Bass frequent do not [usually] permit them to be commanded from the shores, even with the double-handed rod."

Most trout and salmon anglers of the time believed that fly fishing wasn't quite legitimate unless it was done wading or from the bank. Herbert, however, believed you should enjoy the sport you're near when you're not near the sport you prefer. That's why he'd rather fly fish from a boat than merely watch breaking fish from the beach.

Herbert also enjoyed being row-trolled by Charlie Holt. "Almost any small fish will answer for the bait, but the New York shiner, the real smelt, or the atherine—alias sand smelt or spearling[1]—especially the latter, will the most readily allure him. This method of fishing, second only to the use of the fly, is the most exciting, as it requires finer tackle, and consequently calls forth far more skill, than the ordinary modes of fishing for him at the bottom."

Since trolling had its own sporting code that limited the angler to only one—always held—rod, Herbert recommended "for boat fishing, a strong ash or hickory, and lance-wood, rod, with patent guides and the new agate funnel-top, which can be procured at Conroy's [in Manhattan], and is one of the most perfect improvements of the day, with a Salmon-reel and two hundred yards of silk or grass [woven fiber—initially hemp,

[1]There's some confusion here. "Spearling" or "spearing" was a name used along the shores of the New York Bight for the silversides. "Sand smelt," however, most likely referred to another fish known as the sand launce or sand eel. Of the two, Herbert was probably recommending the silversides, since it stays on a hook longer than the softer-bodied sand eel.

later cotton] line, will be found the best; of course, for Salmon fishing, horse[hair] and silk line takes the precedence of all others. A rod of twelve or fourteen feet will suffice from a boat, but for bank or bridge fishing one of about eighteen feet is preferred by the best fishers.

"Comparatively few persons troll for Bass as described above; for, in fact, the great majority, even of our good fishermen, are in some sort pot-anglers, and prefer taking monstrous giants of the water with coarse tackle, to the far greater excitement of skillfully and delicately conquering a moderate-sized fish with the finest tackle. The Striped Bass, it is said, is known to attain the weight of a hundred pounds; but such giants are rare, though up to forty or fifty pounds they are no rarities. The largest fish are taken in deep, rapid tide-ways, such as Hellgate [in New York's East River] or the Haerlem River, by trolling from the stern of a row-boat with a strong hand-line and a large hook baited with that hideous piscine reptile, or insect rather, the real squid,[2] or with the artificial squid of tin or pewter."

The basic design of the tin, pewter, or, today, chromed lead jig dates back to colonial times, when it was developed specifically for such littoral predators as bluefish, weakfish, and striped bass. Such lures could be slung from the beach and hauled hand over hand through schools of feeding fish, or they

---

[2]Squid are neither reptiles nor insects, but cephalopods—highly active and remarkably clever members of the mollusk family. Throughout the nineteenth century, the word *reptile* was freely applied to a spectrum of creatures. Historian-novelist Patrick O'Brian even had his *Post Captain* (1972) hero, Jack Aubrey, describe honeybees as "reptiles."

could be trolled on handlines. It was not until the end of the nineteenth century that reels were developed suitable for metal squid to be cast and retrieved, as they are today. Herbert didn't think much of these lures, since their use requires "more strength than skill and is a very wearisome pursuit."

Herbert was troubled that so many Americans seemed to think angling ethics applied to freshwater fishing only. Some of the very same people who wouldn't dream of selling trout or salmon thought nothing of selling the striped bass they caught. Herbert distinguished between "legitimate or honest fishing" practiced by the amateur for sport, and "professional" fishing practiced by those with a profit motive. He placed rod-and-reel fishing on a higher plane than handlining in part because rod-and-reelers seemed less inclined to sell their catch.

"Nor," he wrote, "can I say that I look with much sympathy on those who fish for [stripers] as is the usual practice at Macomb's Dam, King's Bridge, or Belleville Bridge on the Passaic [in New Jersey], and similar places, with floats and sinkers and the bottom baits. . . .

"In killing the Bass [by sporting means]," Herbert continued, "great skill, great perseverance, and incessant vigilance are necessary. It is a *sine qua non* to keep him up, frustrating his efforts to rush to the bottom, and to hold him ever in hand, with a taut line, ceding nothing to his wildest efforts, except on absolute compulsion.

"Excellent tackle is requisite, and to preserve it excellent, constant attention to it must be had, or all will be in vain. Nothing is more provoking than to lose a fine fish, well played, and perhaps all but killed, owing to some slight imperfection in the gut bottom [i.e., leader] or the arming [i.e., sharpening] of the hooks, which care, before coming to the water's edge, would have easily and surely prevented."

Herbert concluded his striper section in *Frank Forester's Fish and Fishing* by suggesting that spoon lures—first used by Julio Buel in 1834 for black bass and pike—would also work well for striped bass. Eventually, following the Civil War, spoons of all sizes and shapes were designed for striped bass fishing. One of the most effective is the so-called 'bunker spoon, which imitates a large, crippled menhaden. It's ironic that Frank Forester may have sparked interest in developing such a cumbersome trolling lure, since Henry William Herbert so much preferred taking stripers with a fly.

# · 3 ·

# CAPITOL ANGLING

IN 1964, AS a newly commissioned naval ensign, I was posted to the Defense Language Institute in the District of Columbia, where I lived in a top-floor apartment overlooking the U.S. Supreme Court and the Folger Shakespeare Library. Over the next nine months, I wasn't so busy learning Vietnamese that I didn't have time to fish and observe fishing in and around Washington. I saw healthy-looking channel catfish taken from the very unhealthy-looking waters of the Annacostia River, where one of my teachers caught them during his lunch break and kept them alive in a sink in the janitor's closet until it was time to go home. One dawn, I saw a pair of hefty largemouth bass hauled from the tidal basin in front of the Jefferson Memorial by a pair of Pentagon employees, who said they often fished there on their way to work. Throughout the spring of '65, I watched herring pulse up Rock Creek and striped bass roll in the Potomac below Little Falls, while people of every age and complexion used every imaginable kind of tackle to catch them.

Stripers were not as abundant in 1965 as they'd been a century earlier, when the first Joseph Fletcher began renting rowboats to anglers who wanted to fish below Little Falls. That Fletcher's great-grandson was a young man when I first visited his boathouse off Canal Road, but he'd already served many of the celebrated politicians of his time, just as his great-grandfather had served those of his era. John F. Kennedy, for example, and then his brothers Robert and Edward, had bought bait at Fletcher's to fish for white perch and striped bass. The fourteen-foot oak-framed and cypress-planked boats they rented were constructed according to a Fletcher formula dating back to the 1850s.

"I can remember watching my grandfather soaking the cypress boards in the Chesapeake and Ohio Canal behind the boathouse so they could be bent to shape the sides of the boats," recalls the fourth Joe Fletcher today.

The first Fletcher quit in the local iron- and steelworks when he found he could make more money and be more independent by serving the anglers of Georgetown, only half a mile downstream from where he'd bought land for his boathouse. No one knows what the first Fletcher charged to rent a boat, but during the Great Depression, the daily rate was 50 cents. By 1965, the cost had gone up to $1 an hour, or $5 a day. Still, that was a bargain, considering what it offered in the way of a riverine-wilderness experience just fifteen minutes from my apartment on Capitol Hill. As I rowed across the upwelling channel some eighty feet deep off Three Sisters Island and looked across to the Virginia bluffs—where the mostly hidden Washington Memorial Parkway protected the riparian right-of-way from development—it was easy to imagine how the first Fletchers had hunted deer there to live on, along with what they caught in the river. How sensible and farsighted the first Joe Fletcher was to follow his bliss, since few American families can boast of the continuity and contentment of his descendants.

The most significant change in the Potomac since the first Fletcher built his boathouse is not in the river's appearance, but in the quality of its fishing. Atlantic sturgeon—some weighing between 200 and 350 pounds—were regularly recorded from the river below the falls throughout the eighteenth century, and even up to the last decade of the nineteenth. By 1900, however, overfishing of these sturgeon, whose females reach sexual maturity some years later than human females do, meant this species had become threatened with extinction.

Overfishing in the 1880s and '90s also jeopardized striped bass. The Atlantic coastal population collapsed for the first time since Europeans arrived in the New World. Some biologists contend that stripers have always gone though cycles of abundance and scarcity, like those noted for bluefish as far back as 1764. However, the cycles of pelagic-spawning bluefish stem from errant ocean currents and temperatures, not the modern problem of overfishing. There're simply no records indicating that stripers ever seriously declined before the 1890s. Since then, however, the species has twice more declined and recovered, although never quite to the levels before each boom. Landings go up, but they generally reflect increased fishing pressure, not more fish.

The present recovery may not last even as long as the first two, since fisheries administrators seem determined to try the impossible: to please both of their constituencies simultaneously. To make commercial fishermen happy, technicians have fashioned statistical models justifying maximum yields of the most marketable-sized stripers: those eighteen to twenty-four inches long. To make recreational fishermen happy, the technicians have used slightly different models to justify a maximum yield of trophy fish over thirty inches long. The net result (pun intended) is excessive pressure on most adult year-groups.

Such pressure is compounded when hordes of new anglers take up striped bass fishing in response to the biologists' assurance that the species is "fully recovered." When the expanding pressure invariably causes striper stocks to buckle, the anglers blame netters, cycles, weather—almost anything but their own contributions to the overfishing. Many also subscribe to the bureaucratic myth that any increase in striper stocks is a result of subtle management techniques, while decreases are a result of circumstances beyond human control. Ten years ago, however, Marylanders and Virginians learned that the only truly effective management tool is a complete fishing moratorium.

Washington's leading citizens have always been transients. And since politicians produce only opinions and paperwork, the city has escaped much of the more obvious environmental degradation caused by manufacturing and heavy industry elsewhere along the Atlantic Coast. Up until the Vietnam War, the District of Columbia was still closely surrounded by farms and forests as well as the Chesapeake Bay. Its style of life was a paradoxical, but not unpleasant, blend of Yankee hospitality and southern efficiency.

Renting a boat at Fletcher's was like fishing in a time warp. The river between the Chain and Key Bridges made you feel you were fishing outside a small town in another century rather than next to the capital of the most powerful nation on earth. In the spring, golden willows, red maples, and satin-white dogwood blossoms softened the steep banks and rocky islands of the upper gorge. Some anglers anchored or drifted with cut herring, while others slowly paddled or row-trolled spoons and swimming plugs. About the only ingredients missing that would have been there a century earlier were bald eagles and fly fishermen. (The most common birds fishing below the falls today are cormorants and ospreys.)

In the 1960s, most fly fishermen were turned off by the crowds trying to snag-hook or dip-net herring along the shore. Farmers came from miles away with huge dip nets—five or six feet in diameter—to catch herring, which they salted down in crocks and barrels. Increasing numbers of embassy personnel from Asia and Africa joined the farmers and local Washingtonians, so it was sometimes difficult to find elbow room at Little Falls and along Rock Creek.

"My daddy used to do it, too," recalls Joe Fletcher the fourth. "I got so sick of eating salt herring! One time I carried so many gunnysacks of fish up the steep path from the river, it almost broke my back. It took a strong man to fight the raging water during spring floods with those big herring nets. I've seen men sit down exhausted to rest, take a shot of whiskey, and go at it again."

Today, the District of Columbia requires a $5 license for any resident angler between fourteen and sixty-five years of age. Since this license requires no test of angling competency and provides no benefit of superior management, it's a tax, pure and simple. The only "benefit" is in avoiding a fine, but not necessarily a hassle, from one of the D.C. police or federal park rangers who patrol the river and its banks. The $5 license becomes, in effect, the government's equivalent of "protection money."

Maybe that's one reason there're fewer anglers below the falls these days. Another is that shad and striped bass no longer congregate in surface-rippling numbers. Modern fly fishermen are more likely to be found creeping along the banks of the C&O Canal in search of carp than casting streamers for stripers in the Potomac. A few, however, are still there. Some try the falls, not just in hope, but in homage to Daniel Webster, who may have cast flies there to stripers as early as

1813, when he first came to Washington to take his seat in the U.S. House of Representatives. Even after he was appointed U.S. secretary of state in 1841, Webster found time to fly fish for striped bass below Little Falls.

Spencer Fullerton Baird also fly fished the Potomac before the Civil War. He was secretary of the Smithsonian Institution as well as this nation's first fish commissioner, appointed in 1871. In the latter office, he provided some assistance to private citizens who wanted to transplant striped bass to California, but he was also responsible for introducing the carp throughout the United States—a less happy story.

In 1855, Baird contributed several observations on striped bass to the *Ninth Annual Report* of the board of regents of the Smithsonian Institution. Rather than use its scientific name, Baird referred to the striper as the "rockfish." From Georgia to Maryland, and well up the Delaware River, the striper is called the "rock" or "rockfish." How it got this name—seemingly more appropriate to the granite coasts of New England than to the muddy rivers and estuaries of the South—is a mystery, unless the name is linked to the fish's spawning run to the fall line, where water tumbles onto the coastal plain through rocky gaps and over bouldered rapids.

"The rock," Baird noted, "takes a bait readily; and, from the vigor of its actions, affords fine sport with the rod and reel; the fly [is] especially adapted to the capture of this species."

Baird mentioned the adverse impact that dams were having on all anadromous fish, but—being a man of his century—he also believed that dams were necessary "improvements" and no worse than such natural impediments as waterfalls. "The rockfish," he wrote, "is more abundant in Chesapeake bay and its tributaries than anywhere else to the northward. Here they occur all the year round, and are taken in great numbers. During their migration, they feed voraciously upon the herring bound on the same errand up the fresh-water streams. These ascend to a great height, in the Susquehanna, before the dams were built, reaching the forks at Northumberland, and possibly beyond. The falls of the Potomac offer serious impediments to their passage much above the city of Washington. Arrested in this way, they accumulate in considerable numbers, and afford great sport to the citizens of the place during spring and early summer. The late Mr. Webster was frequently to be seen patiently exercising that skill which made him eminent among the celebrated fishermen of the day."

Daniel Webster had died three years earlier, in 1852, after failing to be nominated by the Whig Party as its presidential candidate in that year's election, won by Democrat Franklin Pierce. For decades afterward, Webster was remembered and even revered by those who longed to leaven their careers in public service with ample opportunities to fish. One such politician was Robert Barnwell Roosevelt, who became a role model for his more famous nephew, Teddy. The elder Roosevelt began his outdoor writing career with *Game Fish of the Northern States of America and British Provinces* (1862). He was only thirty-three when this—his first—book was published, and he'd apparently done little fly fishing for stripers. Consequently, he recommended natural bait over artificials and boasted of his "discovery" that the scallop is the best striped bass bait of all: "I took the largest fish under the most unfavorable circumstances with it, when they would not touch the most tempting crab. The heart of the scollop [sic] is pearly white, and is attractive and so good that no wonder the bass should be crazy for it. It is difficult to manage and easily washed off the hook, but if any fisherman shall see bass, as I have often, lying in a deep pool, occasionally leaping out or sluggishly showing their back fins on the surface and refusing all allurements, let him try scollops, and he will think of me in his dying hour."

Striped bass don't free-jump very often, and when they do, they're nearly impossible to tempt with anything. In October 1994, near the fourth island of the Chesapeake Bay Bridge-Tunnel, my frequent fishing companion, Bagley Walker, and I saw more than a dozen eight- to twelve-pound stripers arc low over the glassy calm sea and reenter the water as cleanly as Olympic divers. So long as the fish were feeding in this manner, they were immune to any of the jigs, plugs, or flies we offered. It may be significant that all the fish I've ever seen free-jumping were welterweights. Big stripers are possibly too heavy to jump, and small stripers lack the "authority" to do so.

By 1884, when Roosevelt published *Superior Fishing; Or the Striped Bass, Trout, Black Bass, and Blue-Fish of the Northern States,* he had not only gained greater confidence as an angler and outdoor writer—enough to dare rank the striped bass above the trout in the title of his book—he'd also become a devotee of Potomac fly fishing. This is how he described this once and future fishery and the people who perverted it for profit: "Flyfishing for [striped] bass is the perfection of the sport, and infinitely surpasses in excitement all other modes of killing these noble fish. The best season on the Potomac is in July or August, and the favorite hours the early morning, or the twilight of the evening. The ignorant and mercenary natives who inhabit the romantic region of hill and valley in the neighborhood of Tenally Town, about five miles northwest of Washington, and who, dead to the beauties that nature has lavished around them, and utterly unacquainted with scientific angling, look merely to their two cents per pound for striped bass, manufacture a fly by winding red or yellow flannel round the shank of a large hook, adding sometimes a few white feathers. They substitute for rod a young cedar sapling, denuded of bark and seasoned by age, and attaching to the upper end a stout cord, fish with the large flannel swathed hook in the rapids and below the falls of the Potomac, at the old chain bridge, and without a reel, kill bass of twenty or thirty pounds."

Having expressed his contempt for the "mercenary natives" who lived along Rockville Pike (now Wisconsin Avenue in the District of Columbia), Roosevelt described the aesthetics of Potomac fly fishing: "No spot can be imagined more wild and romantic, and with proper tackle, the reel, the lithe salmon rod, and the artistic fly—no sport can be more exciting. The roar of the angry flood, the bare precipices topped with foliage on the opposite bank, the flat dry bed of the stream where it flows during the heavy freshets, but at other seasons a mass of bare jagged rocks, and the dashing spray of the broken current lend a charm to the scene. While the fish, rendered doubly powerful by the force of the stream, and aided by the numerous rocks and falls, have every chance to escape. . . .

". . . The scientific angler is master of the situation; he can reach any part of the current, casting into the eddies at the base of the precipitous cliffs opposite; he can yield to the rush of the prey; can retire, paying out line, to surer footing, and can follow the fish along the shore; and finally, having subdued his spirit and broken his strength, can lead the prize, gleaming through the transparent water with the sun's rays reflected in rainbow colors from his scales, into some quiet nook where he can gaff him with safety. Such is fly-fishing for striped bass amid the most lovely scenery, gorgeous in its summer dress of green and alternating hill and valley, dotted with pretty farms and smiling grain-fields; and there is but little sport that can surpass it."

In the second half of the nineteenth century, art and science were as two faces of the same cultural coin. This meant that someone who fished with sufficient style, knowledge, capability, and a fly rod was a "complete angler." However, he was less "complete" if he dapped his fly rather than cast it: "Bass are said to be taken with the fly in other rivers of the Southern States, and also to a certain degree in those of the north. At the mouths of narrow inlets, where the tide is rapid and diluted with fresh-water, a gaudy red and white fly with a full body, kept on the surface by the force of the current and not cast as in fly-fishing, will occasionally beguile them; but generally speaking, bass are not fished for with the fly north of the Potomac."

Note that Roosevelt distinguished between "fly fishing" and merely keeping a fly "on the surface by the force of the current." Some modern fly-fishing guides will encourage a novice angler to cast to a piling or jetty and merely jiggle his fly in the current while the guide holds the boat in place with the engine or an anchor. However, that's not fly fishing; it's trolling. And while it may occasionally be a productive way to hook striped bass, it's not the proper way to use a fly rod.

"After a fish is struck," Roosevelt continued, "the same care has to be exercised if he is heavy that is necessary with the salmon, and he will often compel the angler to follow him a long distance ere the gaff[1] terminates the struggle. Bass make very determined but not such rapid runs as their fellow-denizen of the flood, the salmo salar [Atlantic salmon], but rarely retain that reserved force which makes his last dash so often fatal; nevertheless they are resolute and powerful, and have to be handled with care."

A final note on Potomac angling for striped bass comes from Theodore Gordon, the father of modern American fly fishing. Writing in 1913, Gordon noted that "on the same

---

[1]A fringe benefit of size-limit management is that gaffs are no longer legal for striped bass fishing anywhere in the United States. Today, if catch-and-release anglers can't reach into the water and seize a striper by its lower jaw to remove the hook, they can minimize damage to the fish by using a rubber-mesh net.

tackle [the striper] makes longer runs and fights as well as the Atlantic salmon. Large striped bass were at one time fished for at the Falls of the Potomac with large flies. I have killed them [myself] with Bumble-puppy flies."

Note the past tense. On the eve of World War I, Atlantic stripers had not yet recovered from overfishing in the 1890s. When small schools were located, the action was occasionally hot—just as it was during the striper's most recent decades of scarcity, the 1970s and '80s. But the cornucopian age of striped bass angling ended more than a century ago, and each succeeding generation of Joe Fletchers has responded to the growing uncertainty by providing other recreational options at the boathouse. That's why Joe Fletcher the fourth now rents bicycles, not boats, to perennial presidential hopeful Jesse Jackson and his entourage; and when someone does go fly fishing below the falls today, he's more likely to catch a white perch than a striped bass.

# · 4 ·

# BRING THE JUBILEE

LITTLE WAS WHAT it seemed to be in New York City during the Civil War. Even the so-called draft riots of 1863 didn't begin as a protest against military impressment. For years, on July 12, the city's large Irish population had refought the Battle of the Boyne to determine whether, maybe, this time, the Catholics could beat the Protestants. Of course, the original battle was fought in 1690, but New York's Irish Americans were still at it as late as 1872. Invariably, the state militia or local fire brigades had to be called out to quell the rioting, since most of the city's police were Irish and disinclined to arrest other brawling sons of Eire.

By the time the militia arrived on the scene in 1863, the instigators had broadened their agenda to include not just the supposed inequities of the draft, but also the alleged unfairness of having to compete with blacks for blue-collar jobs. Anyone resembling a Protestant, a war supporter, or a Negro was in for it, and dozens were beaten to death or hanged from the nearest lampposts. It was not New York's finest hour.

Yet from July 13 to July 16, local newspapers played down the mayhem and diverted their readers with articles about women's fashions (including tips on how to get in and out of a coach while wearing a bustle without at the same time providing an eyeful for hopeful boys hanging around the depot), the latest horse-racing results from Brooklyn (including a story about the revival of chariot racing there), and when and where the striped bass were biting.

The most popular angling writer in New York during the Civil War was Genio C. Scott. His paternal grandfather had been a colonel in the Revolutionary army and donated nearly a thousand acres due him for military service to the Freemasons of Livingston County (New York), who subsequently built and named the town of Scottsville in his honor. By the time Genio was born in 1809 there was no land left, and the boy watched his father struggle to make ends meet as a teacher. Genio decided he'd rather be rich. Although Scott's father wanted the boy to become a doctor, in those days medicine didn't offer much financial security. Doctoring—like soldiering and ministering—was a respectable but unrenumerative way to serve society, best left to sons with inheritances.

Although he passed his exam for a teacher's certificate at the age of fifteen, young Genio instead became a clerk to a local magnate who owned a farm, a tavern, a grocery, a drugstore, and a tailor shop. Genio took this early business experience into dry goods, switched to canal and railway contracting, and finally became the traveling representative for several New York manufacturing firms. He was smart, industrious, congenial, and a good salesman. He made a lot of money and soon retired to start a new career in publishing.

He contributed a "Ladies' Column" to the *Home Journal,* which subsequently became the *Ladies' Home Journal.* He wrote a monthly fashion page for *Graham's Magazine* and edited two publications of his own, the *Mirror* and *Report of Fashions.* At the same time, he acquired a clothing store and a foundry, and wrote outdoor stories for four different magazines, all of them called *Spirit of the Times.* At one point, the "old" *Spirit of the Times,* the "new" *Spirit of the Times, Wilkes' Spirit of the Times,* and *Porter's Spirit of the Times* were published simultaneously. It was, indeed, a freewheeling era.

Scott thought of himself as a poet as well as a journalist, and he counted among his literary and drinking cronies such luminaries as N. P. Willis, Fitz Greene Hallock, and Edgar Allan Poe. Scott's pedigree, business acumen, and publishing fame made him a celebrity in a city that has always doted on celebrities. As a result, Scott sampled the very best that New York had to offer, including some excellent striped bass angling. In *Fishing in American Waters* (1869)—a book drawn partly from previously published articles—Scott described his outings in a conversational style reminiscent of Izaak Walton. His stories have a rural background difficult to imagine in Greater New York today, and they're haunted by the fact that the bloodiest war in U.S. history had just ended. Yet nowhere in Scott's narrative was there the least hint of it: "In order that the reader may proximately realize the character of the striped bass as a game fish, I propose taking him with me on several excursions after the lustrous beauty. . . . The weather and tide are favorable, and the moon is right for giving fish an excellent appetite and great activity. Fishes in waters near the ocean bite best in the first quarter of the moon, while those which are up rivers and creeks, near fresh water, bite best at full tides, and immediately after a 'nor'-easter,' when the wind, having backed round by the south, has settled in the northwest. You may prove these facts without going a dozen miles from the metropolis."

In the mid–nineteenth century, every good sporting trip to upper Manhattan or the Harlem River began with "a night of sound sleep and an incomparable breakfast" at the Astor Hotel. From there anglers traveled by coach along forested Bloomingdale Road to King's Bridge, which was also the name of a "spicy and succulent oyster" harvested in the Harlem and transported to Dorlan & Schafer's Oyster Saloon near Fulton Market, where the after-theater crowd dined. After overexploitation and pollution destroyed the King's Bridge area, the best oysters came from Blue Point on Long Island.

"We will first see what sport there is to be had at the east bridge," wrote Scott, "where we will joint our rods, and rig sinkers and floats according to the movement of the tide. I perceive that the tide is just on the turn to flood. Rig light for half an hour, and then change to heavier sinker and larger float. I like bridge fishing, for, after making a cast, you may humor your line so as to lead the bait in the most angling manner from current to current; and then, in striking at a bite forty yards off, there is so much sport in playing your fish until you get him into the slack water formed by the piers of the bridge. . . .

"Strike! You've hooked him! There! give him play, but feel his weight, and make him contend for every foot of line you give him, or he will take the whole without exhausting himself, and you will lose him. Do not permit him to run back on you, for that is a favorite dodge of these striped sides to get slack line, and enable them to dislodge the hook. Keep your rod up nearly perpendicular, giving him the benefit of its spring, for he is bony-mouthed, though the teeth in his upper jaw are too small and short to bite or even chafe off a silk-worm gut snell [i.e., leader]. Keep your fish out of the swiftest of the tide, and, after playing him until he succumbs from exhaustion, land him on the shore, for he is too heavy to lift upon the bridge. . . . Now, as the tide has become too swift for float-fishing, just step into this boat, and we will row down to the first island in the creek, seventy-five rods beyond the west bridge, and try Spuyten Duyvel Creek."

With names such as Spuyten Duyvel, Harlem, Staten Island, and the Kills part of every New Yorker's lexicon, it was easy for local fishermen to feel connected to that period when the area was still a Dutch colony. It was easier still when a sportsman had one or more friends of Dutch ancestry as frequent angling companions. Scott's friend Judge Henry

Brevoort owned the block on Fifth Avenue between Eighth and Ninth Streets and kept an inn—the Brevoort House—on the corner of Fifth Avenue and Eighth Street, patronized in particular by captains of English steamers. Despite his work as a magistrate and innkeeper, Henry Brevoort found ample time to fish, and on one occasion, Scott reported, although he himself caught 174 stripers, the judge "beat me by one fish."

Few sport-caught fish were released in the nineteenth century. By the same token, however, few were sold. In the judge's case, what he and Scott caught was usually taken back to the Brevoort House and offered to the guests for dinner. Although some 1860s amateurs probably killed as many striped bass as commercial fishermen did, so long as they did the killing with a rod and reel, rather than a net, they were considered to be "sportsmen." It would take the collapse of Atlantic coastal stripers a quarter century later to start a few anglers thinking that a dead fish is a dead fish, no matter how it's landed.

Scott's next chapter on striped bass was entitled "Trolling in Hell Gate." To the uninitiated, this may sound ominous, and Scott's opening words do little to allay anxiety. But I was not yet a teenager when my father—on a run between Long Island Sound and East Rockaway Inlet by way of the East River—let me take his boat through this famous rip. The swelling current shifted us off-course a couple times, but otherwise the trip was a piece of cake. Naturally, I didn't tell my schoolmates that. All they heard was that I'd taken a boat by myself through the notorious Gate of Hell.

"When you decide to troll for a day over the tumultuously-seething and hissing waters of Hell Gate, where an oarsman must know the tides and shoals to keep his boat right side up, you will require heavier tackle. . . . The reel should carry 600 feet of hawser-laid linen line, of from twelve to fifteen threads, thus rendering it about the size of a fine salmon line; but the line should be free from any oily composition, and a dip in dye to give it a greenish shade is beneficial. Never, by any chance, use a check reel for coast or estuary fishing. Depend on the pressure of your thumb for checking the fish, and wear knitted thumb-stalls."[1]

In contrast to Robert Barnwell Roosevelt, who liked angling by himself, Genio Scott preferred having a guide who'd do almost everything but hook and play the fish. "Those who employ a man to row and gaff the fish," he wrote, "would do well to direct him to squid half a dozen hooks [i.e., rig up half a dozen extra baits] before starting, and lay them aside in the boat under some wet rock-weed before leaving shore. If you have ever been trolling—as I have—when large bass were biting generously, you will realize the force of this advice. It is unpleasant to be trolling in rough waters, and, when a bass

---

[1]For nearly a century, the best fishing lines were made of woven linen. Each thread tested at two pounds breaking strength dry, and three pounds wet. When the International Game Fish Association was founded in 1939, a twelve-thread line was classified at thirty-six pounds test, and a fifteen-thread line at forty-five pounds test. Although the lines were "hawser-laid," they were not as thick as the word implies. Linen lines were often dyed some darker color to make them presumably less perceptible to the fish. Cotton lines were usually darkened by dipping them in tar, which also retarded rotting. A check reel had a simple brake, of little value in playing a fish.

strikes the back of your hook and takes your bait without fastening, to be obliged to stop and squid a hook [i.e., rig up another squid] before proceeding.

"Now for the fray! Our boats are made by Hughes, fellow-apprentice of George Steers;[2] and with Sile Wright and Sandy Gibson as guides and gaffers, we shall be sculled over all the favorite trolling grounds from the ferry below to the Drowned Marsh above Ward's Island."

One of the more productive locations in Hell Gate was Holt's Rock, and there was a particular technique to fishing it: "'Swinging a rock' is done by the oarsman holding the boat sixty feet from the rock and swinging it so that the troll [i.e., bait] will move about the rock on all sides and play as if alive. This art is possessed in great perfection by Hell Gate oarsmen."

Scott lost the largest striped bass he ever hooked while swinging Holt's Rock: "As my squid was struck by [the fish], Sile said he heard the rod crack. But the fish made such a long, vigorous run, that I scarcely realized what he said, and, after turning the fish and reeling him in gradually, he broke water with a leap, clearing the surface, and revealing a forty-pounder. [Other than this one reference, I've never seen nor heard of a really big striper jumping clear of the surface, especially when hooked. Still, this is Scott's story, and he contin-

---

[2]George Steers was the best-known American shipbuilder of his day. He crafted hulls for the Collins Line, Cunard's American rival on the lucrative round-trip runs between New York and Liverpool. Collins's ships were named for seas, including the Steers-built Queen of the Fleet, the *Adriatic*. Transatlantic travel was still a dangerous undertaking in the mid–nineteenth century, and two Collins liners, the *Arctic* and the *Pacific*, were lost in the decade prior to the Civil War—the latter with everyone aboard and not a clue as to what happened.

ued:] While turning and bringing him toward the boat for the third time, he darted down and snapped the middle joint of my rod in two. When I threw the broken rod down at my feet and took hold of the line, the fish made but feeble resistance, and I towed him alongside the boat and shouted to Sile for the gaff, but he had thoughtlessly placed it in the other boat. I then endeavored to put my hand in [the fish's] mouth, and, while in the act, the fish turned over, breaking the hook and bleeding profusely as he settled off into the tide, leaving us astonished and almost desperate. On examination, I learned that a flaw in the hook had been the cause of our loss of the fish; but had we rowed ashore and towed the fish after the rod broke, we should probably have landed him. I have never since been caught trolling or angling for large bass without a gaff and tried [i.e., tested] hooks."

Despite this bitter disappointment, Scott soon recovered his usual equanimity: "With broken rod and tangled line, I ordered Sile to row away from the scene of our misfortune. I found my friend [in another boat] at Hammock Rocks, his [twenty-pound] fish laid out in state of rock-grass, and he mutely bending over it with a face radiant with pleasurable satisfaction at his achievement. Trolling, to him, was a new-born pleasure, and his first capture a trophy of which a slayer of lions might be justly proud. . . .

"Having toasted the health and appetite of bass in that neighborhood in a glass of sherry, and replaced the broken joint of my rod with a sound one, we again seated ourselves in our boats, and commenced trolling the Little Gate, the Kills, and all about Randall's and Ward's Islands, and, after the usual alternatives of hopes, fears, and moments of ecstasy, we finished up a mess[3] of seven bass between us, the largest nearly thirty, and the smallest four pounds in weight."

Striped bass may still be caught in occasional abundance in the East River and lower New York Harbor—as a family of doctors has shown time and again over the past half century. Nick Lyons described an outing with the patriarch, Dr. Ben Sherman, and one of his four physician-sons in the *New York Times* on November 25, 1985. Nick was pledged to secrecy as to where precisely they fished, but he did say they caught two-foot stripers almost as fast as their jigs and bucktails could reach bottom somewhere "in the region of the Statue of Liberty."

Despite the frenetic action, Nick was clearly uncomfortable jigging for stripers. "There was an art to this jigging business," he wrote, "and I was far from mastering it. Though I'd done my share of bottom bouncing when I was a kid, I'd long since lost my heart to a slender shaft of bamboo and a hat full of feathers, and my absorption in the complexity of such a love had wrecked any skill I'd had at bottom fishing. I had to reconcile myself at once to the sad fact that I made a poor jigger of diamond jigs."

Still, it's also evident Nick was having a ball: "Gary did most of the boat work. . . . He was sighting on Lady Liberty, all braced for her operation [a major renovation of the statue was

---

[3]*Mess* is the proper term for a number of freshly caught fish, just as *bag* is the correct term for a number of freshly killed gamebirds.

42

undertaken at about this time], and on a building among the many that rose like monoliths behind us, and on this and that, and he'd tool uptide, into a flock of birds, cut the motor, and then drift with the tide. The New York City skyline was majestic and jagged and looming; craft large and small kept horning us; the sonar showed black; and the five of us would drift downtide, our diamond jigs and bucktails working in the depths of lower New York Bay."

Almost as spectacular as the scenery was the paradox of fishing mere minutes from the hurly-burly of the world's greatest city. When Nick told his hosts he had to go, they made one more drift, caught one more fish apiece, and changed into business attire during their dash to the South Street Seaport. "On the way," Nick recalled, "through the rows of smaller buildings, I thought I caught a glimpse of Fraunces Tavern, above which, members of the Anglers' Club would already be gathering for some talk about last year's dry-fly fishing on the Beaverkill. . . .

"Since it was New York, no one but a few tourists even noticed the two of us [Dr. Gary Sherman and Nick] climbing off the boat and marching past the shops, chattering about the past three hours' work. Gary said he'd be in the operating room in ten minutes. I hopped a cab and was fifteen minutes early for my lunch date on 23rd Street—but I stank a little, all day, from striped bass."

More than 130 years earlier, Genio C. Scott had sometimes carried the same smell into the offices of the *Ladies' Home Journal*.

## · 5 ·

# THE JERSEY SHORE

STRIPED BASS OWN the surf. False albacore and bluefish may charge a beach, but their frantic movements express anxiety at being in such surging, shallow water. Other species—notably weakfish in the North, and red and black drum in the South—are comfortable near shore, but they don't cruise in and out of the breakers with quite the élan of striped bass.

Bill Feinberg, my son Christopher, and I had been fishing from the beach at Deal, New Jersey, for less than ten minutes when I saw a striper's fin rise through a breaking wave. The fish continued cruising parallel to the beach even as the wave boiled into foam around it. The fin was in view for just an instant, but the fish's supreme indifference to the sea's energy caused hair to rise on the nape of my neck.

Ten minutes later, while standing in the wash and holding my rod tip high to keep the line free of grass driven inshore by the previous day's storm, I felt a momentary slackness. I struck, took two steps back and struck again. The fish was more puzzled than panicked. It shook its head, then methodically ground thirty yards of line off the reel. It swam down the beach in the direction of three pilings standing in the breakers. I put additional finger pressure on the spool and waded sideways, away from the pilings and the fish.

A friend and occasional angling companion, Frank Mather—who back in the 1950s developed the "M" tag used in marine research to track pelagic gamefish—feels the striped bass is the most overrated sportfish in the world. He prefers bluefin tuna. While there's no question that tuna grow larger, swim faster, and in some other respects are more spectacular than stripers, context is everything. The same striper that wrestles and rolls in confusion when hooked from a trolled boat—especially one whose skipper only slows, but doesn't stop, the engine—will stubbornly and skillfully resist a surf fisherman's every effort to bring it ashore.

The largest striper my father ever landed weighed forty-eight pounds. She engulfed a 'bunker spoon at the end of a weighted wire line while we were trolling one night in the late autumn of 1954. The fish swam straight to the boat. When I shined a light on her, she stayed close to the hull like a whale calf huddled next to its mother. When I gaffed her, she barely struggled. Dad helped me haul her over the transom and flop her into the fishbox where, after a few yawns, she expired. I would have thought her sick, except her roe sacs were already ripening for the following spring's spawning. Thus, we'd compounded the crime of killing a capital breeder by doing so trolling, and with tackle that never allowed the fish to use her instinctive knowledge of waves and near-shore currents.

By contrast, although the Deal fish probably weighed a fifth of Dad's Grande Dame, it contested every yard of line, motivated by its fear of stranding. The striper veered from the pilings, and I recovered ten yards; it curved offshore, and I lost twenty. Suddenly the line went slack. I stumbled back through the suds, reeling like mad. I was just as suddenly jerked forward when the fish reversed course. Then I saw the striper framed in a wave like a mounted specimen in a glass case. The wave tumbled in on itself, and I lost ten yards.

I noticed Bill and Christopher intently watching their own lines. The roar of the surf smothered my heaven-sent yell: "Praise You for another day! Thank You for another fish! But if it's not asking too much, would You let my son hook one?"

The gods are fickle. Not only didn't they grant Christopher a fish, the next moment, my striper was gone, and we hooked nothing else that dawn. Bill's ninety-four-year-old friend, James Thomas Lambie, didn't believe the gods had anything to do with it.

"Stripers are just like other schooling fishes," said Jim. "Lose one, and you lose those that follow the lost fish away. If you have only a few stripers working a section of beach, the loss of even one fish may finish the fishing for that tide. That's something catch-and-release advocates don't often consider.

We should all release more of what we catch. But anglers will have to accept the fact that they'll lose a certain percentage of potential action every time they let a fish go. That's especially true of really big stripers, which only travel in pairs and trios."

Jim Lambie, Bill Feinberg, and other surf fishermen of the North Jersey coast are heirs to a tradition reaching back to 1888 when James Adam Bradley, founder of the town of Asbury Park, and nine of his angling cronies started the area's first fishing club. Developer Bradley donated four rocking chairs and a big brass bell to the pier he built at the south end of Asbury Park. Whenever a club member caught a striped bass there, its weight was rung on the bell—one chime per pound—and, whenever they heard twenty or more chimes sound across the water, everybody from bootblacks to doctors would stop work and run down to see the big fish.

Within two years, the club was called the Monmouth County Protective Association. Its stated purpose was "to prevent the useless waste of fish and to assist in breeding game fish." By 1902, the association had grown so large that it could afford its own pier-based clubhouse and a new name: the Asbury Park Fishing Club. Its constitution redefined the old club's purposes: "To protect saltwater game fish, to create good fellowship and to promote the interest of anglers."

The club was open to anyone "of good moral character." Dues were nominal, and social position and sex were not limiting factors to membership. Although women members were technically part of the ladies' auxiliary, they were entitled to the same prizes as the men. Indeed, some very impressive catches were made by women in the early days and long before it was considered appropriate behavior for women to participate in activities that entailed strength and danger, such as occasionally occur when one fishes all night from a storm-racked beach.

Although my paternal roots lie across the New York Bight in Brooklyn, I feel a kinship with the early Asbury Park Fishing Club because so many of its members were of German extraction. Following the Franco-Prussian War (1870–71) and Prince Otto von Bismarck's persecution of anyone (especially Catholics) who protested his authoritarian policies or who merely wanted to be left alone, waves of immigrants from Central Europe arrived in the United States. Bismarck prosecuted his *Kulturkampf* from 1872 to '79, but it left scars—and encouraged emigration—up to the eve of World War I, when all emigration was stopped to prevent draft-aged men from leaving Germany.

Many Central Europeans settled in Baltimore, New York, and other industrial centers, where their technical skills, willingness to work, and pride in craftsmanship provided them with easy access to the middle class, sometimes mere months after stepping off the ships from Hamburg. By 1897, German accents were so familiar to urban newspaper readers that Rudolph Dirks (1877–1968) could create an instantly popular cartoon strip called *The Katzenjammer Kids* featuring fractured *Deutsch,* two boys named *Hans und Fritz* who were always in trouble (often because they'd rather be fishing than in school), and a rolling-pin-wielding *über Mutter.* The strip was still going strong in the 1940s, when I read it each Sunday for clues to my own antecedents.

My brothers and I were surrounded by such clues. Our father-physician could have fished with men "of a better class," as my mother put it—meaning some of the old family/old money neighbors we were surrounded by after (at my mother's urging) she and Dad moved their infant family to Forest Hills Gardens. But Dad was the son of immigrants, and he felt comfortable with folks who, like him, spoke a little Hungarian, Italian, or Polish, and a lot of German. He opened his office at 6 A.M. and closed it at 11 P.M. to make sure that his mostly blue-collar patients could see him. That's why his fishing companions were more likely to have names like "Schmalhofer" and "Wagonblast" than be the second cousin of Woodrow Wilson, who lived across the street.

At Christmas, we Reiger boys were the only kids on Puritan Avenue who got a house call from Santa Claus. Santa would stroll down the middle of the street, ringing his bell and calling out Christmas greetings in Katzenjammerized English. After he delivered our toys and hugged us *Kinder,* Santa vanished and Herr Unimann appeared to help us assemble our new trains and show us how to load a cap pistol. Yet, unless some part of the house needed repainting, I don't recall seeing Herr Unimann any other time of the year.

Such memories return when I look over early rosters of the Asbury Park Fishing Club. Prominent members included Christian W. Feigenspan, owner of the Feigenspan Breweries in Newark; Jacob Wertheim, who, in addition to catching the largest striped bass of the 1914 and '15 seasons, caught a world-record bluefin tuna (286 pounds) in 1915; A. C. Steinbach, the department store magnate; A. F. "Gus" Meisselbach, manufacturer of the Meisselbach "Quick Takapart" reel; and John A. Seger, tackle store proprietor and creator of the greenheart surf-casting rod.

German Americans were among the most competitive members in the club. When Frank Henes established the New Jersey state record for striped bass in 1913 with a fish weighing precisely fifty-five pounds, his good friend and fellow club member Abe Flavell couldn't rest until he broke that record with a fish weighing fifty-eight pounds, three ounces.

In the 1925 club yearbook, Frank G. "Buck" Ernst, Charles Gulick, John C. Muller, Frank Sinsinger, William H. Schwartz, and J. H. Wortman and his daughter, "Miss Wortman," are among those cited for having won the Gold Button for a striped bass of twenty-five pounds or more; Bela C. Clapp, H. Heinsheimer, Sidney Kohn, Nelson J. Schoen, E. H. Snedeker, John Vogler, and George W. Yetman are listed for winning the Silver Button for a striped bass of fifteen to twenty-five pounds; and Allan Hoffman, A. J. Detsch, William Ehman, A. J. Gude, W. D. Knecht, W. Kuster, Harry W. Metz, Theodore C. Mertz, and William H. Scheffler are all listed as winning a Bronze Button for a striper of ten to fifteen pounds.

Unlike the case of some other early angling fraternities, I find no hint of prejudice anywhere in the history of the Asbury Park Fishing Club. Indeed, it would be difficult from the membership lists to determine which German Americans were

THE STRIPED BASS CHRONICLES

Protestant, Catholic, or Jewish. And just as German American Jewish kids in the Greater New York area grew up learning Christmas carols, my brothers and I grew up learning such wonderfully potent Yiddish words as *gonif* ("thief"), *meiskeit* ("ugly"), and *schlemiel* ("fool").

One of the pleasures in reading old club yearbooks is noting how many angling batons were lovingly passed from one generation to the next. In the case of the Seger family, Arthur told this story of his dad:

"Once when I was late for Sunday school, the minister inquired the cause.

"'I was going fishing,' I said, 'but father wouldn't let me.'

"'That's the right kind of a father to have,' replied the reverend gentleman. 'Did he explain why he didn't let you go?'

"'Yes, sir. He said there wasn't bait enough for two.'"

Probably the best-known member of the Asbury Park Fishing Club was the only child and heir to a Pennsylvania Dutch mining fortune. For many hopeful years, Percy Heilner called his company "Percy Heilner & Son." But the son, Van Campen Heilner, never took much interest in the family business, which, at its peak, owned significant coal seams in Pennsylvania and West Virginia and had offices in half a dozen cities from Cincinnati to London, England.

Heilner was a sickly boy whose parents moved to the Jersey Shore after doctors suggested the sun and salt air might cure the boy's chronic anemia. They did. Van flourished at the Shore and determined he'd always live so he'd never be far or long from the ocean's healing powers. Much of what Heilner knew about surf fishing he learned "down Barnegat way." Some of the regulars there came east from Philadelphia rather than south from Asbury Park. In 1889, Philadelphian A. M. Spangler, president of the Angler's Association of Eastern Pennsylvania, observed that "although the sea—or any salt water—is not less than from fifty to seventy-five miles from Philadelphia, so many are the lines of communication with it, so rapid the transit and so reasonable the fare, that places even more than a hundred miles away, may properly be classed under the head of 'near-by' fishing localities. The nearest points, as Atlantic City, Somers Point, and Ocean City, can be reached in from ninety to a hundred minutes, the first named by three [rail]roads, the latter by one—the West Jersey. By taking one of the earliest morning trains, either of the places named is reached by it in time to afford the angler, who has but a single day for a fishing outing, six or eight hours sport and ample time to secure a home passage by the latest train."

In *The Call of the Surf* (1920), the first book ever devoted entirely to the sport of surf fishing, Heilner wrote, "I love the sea, if only to stand, and gaze at its great, majestic splendor.

"I once fell into conversation with an old fisherman along the beaches, and together we stood for several hours looking at the surf.

"'You know,' he remarked, 'the waves remind me of our lives. Some of 'em comes up to the beach higher 'n others and makes their mark, some of 'em don't git nowheres a-tall. But no matter whether they makes their mark, er fails absolute, they all gotta return to where they come from.'

"Which seemed to me pretty good philosophy."

Despite making a mark "higher 'n others," Heilner never forgot how much he owed older club members such as Gus Wittkamp, George Geiss, Phil Mayer, Gus Meisselbach, and Hartie I. Phillips. They'd adopted a frail youth and helped him become a strong and confident man and our best recorder of marine angling's Golden Age. Heilner was something of a prodigy. He contributed articles to the *American Angler, Field and Stream*—the logotype of this magazine went back and forth, with and without an ampersand, several times during its formative years, until March 1923, when the ampersand became permanent—*Motor Boat, National Sportsman,* and *Sports Afield* before he was out of his teens, and he published *The Call of the Surf* at age twenty-one. *Adventures in Angling* followed two years later. It was derived largely from other articles he'd sold to *Field and Stream, Motor Boat, National Geographic, Recreation,* and *Wide World.*

Also, by the time he was twenty-three, he was an associate editor of *Field and Stream* (still without an ampersand) and a field representative in ichthyology for the American Museum of Natural History. On behalf of the museum, he collected specimens on expeditions to Peru and Ecuador in 1924–25, to Alaska in 1927, and to Cuba in 1934–35. After his first trip to Bimini in 1921, during which he collected several previously unknown fish from the reef, his friend and scientific alter ego, Dr. J. T. Nichols, named two of the new species respectively for Heilner (*Labrisomus heilneri*) and his boat (*Eupomacentus nepenthe*).

"I named her [Nepenthe]," Heilner wrote in *The Call of the Surf*, "after a magic potion used by the ancient Egyptians to make them forget their cares and misfortunes, and well has she proved her name." Unfortunately, Heilner used more mundane potions to forget his own cares and misfortunes and suffered the usual consequences of alcoholism, including a shorter than average life.

In 1937, he published a definitive study of marine angling entitled, simply, *Salt Water Fishing*. The book became angling's first best-seller since Izaak Walton's *The Compleat Angler*. It went through three printings before the end of the year, and six more by 1940.

In September 1943, shortly before he was to report for induction into the U.S. Army, seventeen-year-old Bill Feinberg took his copies of *Salt Water Fishing* and *The Call of the Surf* to Heilner's Spring Lake mansion to have the famous fisherman autograph them. Today, the Heilner home, known as Halbregt, is separated from the old caretaker's cottage by three blocks of multimillion-dollar residences, but during the war it still lay beyond the cottage (another million-dollar residence today) at the end of a long, winding, wooded road. Bill and Van's mutual friend, "Buck" Ernst, had arranged the meeting, but Heilner had to leave town that morning, and Bill left the books with Heilner's mother. Bill was in basic training by the time Heilner returned and signed the books.

Twenty-two years later—long after Bill had survived the Battle of the Bulge, graduated from Cornell University and its law school, and become president of the Asbury Park Fishing

Club—he invited Heilner to speak at the club banquet in January 1965. On that occasion, Heilner updated his autographs in Bill's book, adding: "A little older but still chasing fish, VCH."

Unfortunately, Heilner had few fish-chasing days left. He died two years later. Yet he left a legacy of some of our best outdoor writing. This, for example, is how he described what it means to be a surf fisherman: "Surf fishing is to saltwater angling what trout fishing is to fresh water. It is a one-man game from start to finish. You are the one and only factor. Here you are and there he is. If he runs out all the line, you can't pick up the oars or start the engine and follow him. No cushion or comfortable seat or chair supports your fundament, no thwarts against which to brace your feet, no companion to assist you or guide you. You must find your quarry yourself; you must rig and bait your hook yourself; you must become proficient in the art of casting so you may reach him; and you must bring him through a line of foaming breakers and singing tides until at last, whipped to a standstill, he lies gasping on the wet sands at your very feet.

"Then you must let him go because he deserves it."

# THE SILVER RUSH

"OWING TO THE ideal climate and general food conditions, it is safe to say that the striped bass of California grows more rapidly than do their brothers on the Atlantic side. This may be reasoned from the average catch in the surf as compared with that on the Atlantic side."

Writing in August 1924, A. H. McCloud of Stockton, California, had just finished twenty days of fishing from the beaches of Monterey Bay. On every tide he'd caught one or two stripers whose average weight was precisely twenty pounds. This size, typical for California stripers, boggled the minds of Atlantic coastal anglers, and many remained skeptical. Yet writer and artist Russell Chatham remembers an old newspaper clipping from the *San Raphael Independent Journal* showing a man standing next to a *ninety-pound* striped bass caught on a clam in the delta area north of San Pablo Bay.

In 1920, A. H. McCloud contributed most of the chapter entitled "By Western Seas" to Van Campen Heilner and Frank Stick's *The Call of the Surf*. A melancholy aspect of this book is how relatively little there is in it about striper fishing. Channel bass, even sharks are featured—Stick's frontispiece depicted a surf fisherman hooked to a leaping shark—but "By Western Seas" is the only chapter devoted exclusively to striped bass. This is indicative of the fact that Atlantic stripers had not yet recovered from a secondary population collapse from over-fishing during World War I. Meanwhile, the remote California population was flourishing.

Although Heilner had been to California to fish for marlin off Catalina and salmon off Monterey, he never tried the local surf fishing because he couldn't find anyone who knew any-thing about it.

"Surf fishing?" Californians would ask. "You mean the surf fish—the ones they catch from the piers and rowboats?"

"No," Heilner replied, "I didn't mean those little fellows. . . . A few anglers with whom I conversed were of the impression that one might take fish from the beach, but it was all so vague."

For most Californians, that vagueness continued into the 1970s. When I taught surf casting at Asilomar in the summer of '73, I brought all the rods and reels I'd need, but since my airline overweight charges were high enough, I didn't bring any sinkers—figuring I'd at least be able to pick those up locally. I was wrong. West Coast anglers fish from boats, and store proprietors stared blankly when I asked for leads designed for surf fishing. I did manage to purchase a packet of small cotton tobacco pouches, which my students filled with pebbles and sand and used as expendable "breakaway" weights when they fished from rocky promontories.

I wrote a story about that experience for the June 1974 issue of *Field & Stream*. I remarked that there were three ingredients in the program's success: "First, as members of the National Wildlife Federation, all students came with a great love and interest in the outdoors and an understanding that catching fish wasn't the only pleasure in greeting the dawn waist deep in the surging Pacific. Second, the total Federation program—involving courses in beach ecology, life in the tide pools, sea weeds, shore birds as well as demonstrations in outdoor camping and cooking, and wilderness medicine—acted to reinforce particular elements within the program. For instance, students in the beach ecology course learned how to locate sand crabs—which they could then use as bait in my surf-casting course. And lucky anglers who caught fish while surf casting would rush from my class up to Warren and Ruth Kelly's cooking class in the dunes to see how to prepare a cabezone or surf perch, and then taste its excellent flavor before the fish was half an hour out of the sea. Finally, there's nothing like actually catching fish to make anglers out of beginners. Fortunately, we managed to catch fish in each of my two-hour classes but one—and even in that exception, an angler managed to bring a large cabezone into the surf where classmates saw it flopping about before it got off the hook. . . .

"Brice Halsey, 11-year-old son of the president of the Oklahoma Wildlife Federation, borrowed one of my outfits for a little 'after school' practice. He decided to cast a six-inch silver spoon from the rocks. He hooked a big fish which, according to eye witnesses who still argue about it, was either a striped bass or a salmon. Whatever it was, the monster got away. Undaunted, young Halsey went back day after day—but never got another strike. When I tried to console him toward the end of his stay, he said,

" 'That's all right. I'll be back next year.' "

Unfortunately, there was no next year. The federation's accountants decided that profits at Asilomar were too slim to stage another summit there. Such penny-wise, pound-foolish thinking is even more common today. For instance, few outdoor magazines with national circulations will run a surf-casting story. There's just "not enough product" in it to satisfy advertisers who want readers to buy boats and all the accessories that go with them. As a result, the subtle satisfaction of surf fishing is largely unknown to young anglers.

Not far north of Asilomar, the Salinas River once flowed into Monterey Bay with sufficient volume to constitute an estuary. Farther north and, to use Heilner's words, "a few miles beyond the point where the Salinas River blends its flow with the sapphire waters [of Monterey Bay] is Elkhorn Slough. At both these places the tide ebbs and flows with much force, creating miniature tide rips. Here is a favorite haunt for striped bass."

To give eastern anglers some idea of western surf fishing, Heilner excerpted several days of McCloud's angling diary. This is part of the entry for August 10, 1920: "Fished Elkhorn up until noon but did not have a touch of anything. This rather discouraged us [McCloud and his father], so we decided to try the mouth of the Salinas River. Immediately our luck changed. The bass began striking in good shape. Took two before one o'clock.

"Cooked some lunch on the beach. Had a nice striper broiled over the coals, with some fried potatoes and bread and jam. I don't care if I never see the smoke of a city again! I could stay out here forever!

"Started in right after lunch again. The conditions were ideal. Just a slight ripple on the sea and in the mouth of the river and the bass acted as if they hadn't had any food for a month. We received about three strikes to every fish landed." A friend joined them and soon hooked a striper forty-eight inches in length, twenty-eight inches in girth, and weighing forty-one pounds. McCloud concluded: "These are the kind of fish that make life worth while!"

Despite McCloud's enthusiasm and Heilner's publicity, surf fishing never caught on in the West. The reason, as noted by Leon David Adams—remembered less today as a master angler than as a master viticulturist and the author of the *Wine Handbook Series*—in his *Striped Bass Fishing in California and Ore-*

*gon* (1953), is that "the turbulent, noisy ocean, the smell of salt spray, and the thrill of casting with a powerful surf rod are the things the persistent surf fisherman really loves. He would have to love them, because except when the beaches are visited occasionally by a bass run, surf fishing produces fewer bass per fisherman per season than the other methods used in the Western Striperland."

Had Pacific striper populations held up to what they were at the turn of the century, West Coast surf fishing might have become comparable to what it was, and still is, along some areas of the Atlantic Coast. Starting in the 1930s, however, California stripers began to decline due to the destruction of that arid state's few estuaries. Recreational landings picked up after World War II, but this was due to escalating angling pressure, not because California stripers had found new places to spawn and develop as fingerlings. More people were simply tapping the same limited stocks. Despite stringent conservation measures—at least by East Coast standards—the delicate equilibrium between anglers and striped bass in California was finally broken in the early 1970s, and the fishery rapidly faded over the next decade.

Meanwhile, California stripers had moved up the coast to establish reproducing populations in Oregon's Coos Bay and the Umpqua estuary. That happened so long ago, it's difficult for West Coast anglers to imagine that stripers were once so abundant they even strayed as far north as Washington State.

"We once tagged over a hundred thousand stripers annually to make population estimates and keep tabs on harvest rates," recalls senior fisheries biologist Don Stevens of the California Department of Fish and Game. "We averaged ten thousand returns a year, but got only one return ever from Oregon, and that fish was found floating by someone who salvaged it for crab bait. As California's population of stripers contracted, Oregon's evolved into a separate stock."

Reese Bender of Oregon's Department of Fish and Wildlife notes the consequences: "The Coos Bay population currently numbers only about five hundred to a thousand spawning-sized adults. Of those, up to thirty-five percent are hermaphrodites. That's a sure sign of inbreeding. The affected fish don't live more than about three years as a result of egg binding."

Oregon could revitalize its stocks with new striper genes from the Atlantic. Unfortunately, the Endangered Species Act now prevents both Oregon and California from doing any such thing. Although the striped bass has been in the West for over a century and is in trouble for the same reason that several races of Pacific salmon are—namely, diminished or degraded spawning and nursery habitat—the West Coast striper is still considered to be an exotic species, and the National Marine Fisheries Service (NMFS) has ordered that it be sacrificed to save the salmon.

Ironically, this federal mandate comes only a few years after California initiated a program to rescue young stripers caught on cooling water intake screens and in irrigation pumps. Some twenty-eight thousand stripers were recovered, moved to holding pens, and released in 1992; thirty-four thousand in 1993; more than one hundred thousand in 1994. Plans for half a million were in the works for 1995 and '96 when NMFS determined that insufficient numbers of winter-run chinook salmon were returning to the San Francisco Bay ecosystem to allow the release of any more parr-eating stripers. Striped bass mitigation was put on hold.

Oregonians have ample numbers of chinook salmon in most of their rivers, but too few coho. In order to protect declining coho stocks, the state established a cap of twenty-five thousand striped bass for the Coos Bay estuary. Since the Coos Bay striper population is so far below that, Oregon biologists haven't yet had to make any of the existential choices between striped bass and salmon faced by their California colleagues.

No state biologist in the West believes that salmon can be restored by sacrificing stripers. Anglers and biologists alike realize that salmon and stripers have coexisted along the Pacific Coast for over a century without adversely impacting one another. They also realize that degraded habitat is the core problem for all estuarine-dependent fish in the West, including such important forage species as the now threatened Delta smelt. However, unable to do anything about too many people demanding too much fresh water, federal fisheries administrators have decided to hobble, if not eliminate, the exotic but highly adaptable striped bass in order to "save" the native but far more fragile salmon.

Oregon's striper fishery may be small, but it played an important role in the history of saltwater fly fishing when, in September 1948, outdoor writer Joe Brooks caught a twenty-nine-pound, six-ounce striped bass in Coos Bay to establish a twelve-pound-test-tippet record for the species. Brooks's catch was the equivalent of Columbus being given credit for discovering the New World. Asian immigrants, whose descendants are known as Native Americans, were here first, and Vikings were probably the first Europeans to see the New World. But Columbus's voyages publicized the existence of America, and that made all the difference. Likewise, although we have ample archival evidence that stripers were fished for with flies throughout the nineteenth century, and some very big fish were taken, Brooks's record excited the angling world's imagination in a way that the less-well-publicized catches of the past did not.

Ironically, eight years before Brooks's notable catch, this letter by Maximillian Foster appeared in the *New York Herald Tribune* on November 18, 1940: "How many fly fishermen know that the striped bass may be taken as readily with the fly as . . . other fish? There is nothing new under the sun. There is nothing new in this. I have been fishing for stripers with a fly for the last twenty years. So had the late George Bonbright—for that matter, so have a few others. The curious thing about it is, however, that while, to my knowledge, fishing for striped bass with a fly was practiced more than seventy years ago, for some reason it lapsed into the discard until a few of us caught on again. [The reason for the "lapse into the discard" was the overfishing and subsequent failure of Atlantic coastal stocks in the 1890s.] And that there is nothing intricate nor mysterious in taking stripers by this method is immediately evident, once it has been tried. . . .

"Any angler capable of laying out thirty feet of line stands as good a chance of success as the caster capable of rapping out 70 or 90 or 100 feet—that is, provided he knows where to look for his fish and can get over them. And take it from those who know, a ten, fifteen or twenty-pound striper raised, hooked and fought on a seven-ounce or eight-ounce fly rod puts over an experience calculated to thrill to the marrow the most blasé, calloused hand at fishing. . . . I have a definite feeling that if this type of striped bass fishing were more generally known and practiced, the fact that it was, would put an unbeatable weapon in the hands of the Davids fighting the Goliath of selfish interests who, if not fought, may eventually destroy a great game fish."

Today, Bonbright's 1930s catch of a twenty-six-pound striper on a fly is unremembered, while Brooks has been immortalized for a fish less than four pounds larger and caught a decade later. Yet Brooks himself was less interested in the record as such than in the fact that he'd caught the fish on a balsa-wood popper made to order by Bill Upperman of Atlantic City, New Jersey. Upperman marketed a line of Brooks's bucktail streamers and poppers, and jealous anglers had spread rumors that Brooks had caught the fish "by mistake" on an unknown pattern.

"Why can't they get it right?" grumbled Joe, who wasn't normally a grumbler. "Jimmie Christianson was there guiding us, and our party included Joe Bates,[1] Don Harger, and Chan Brown. It was a white popper, and on that afternoon I hooked another bass at least as big as the first one—maybe bigger."

As a Marylander, born and bred, Brooks had been fly fishing for rockfish since he was a young man. He publicized his catch to encourage more anglers to try this kind of fishing for stripers. If they used the Brooks line of Upperman flies and poppers in the process, so much the better. But the record itself meant little to Joe. It was merely the means of restoring the striper to its preeminence as a fly-rod fish.

The International Game Fish Association now recognizes seven tippet classes, from two pounds to twenty. Furthermore, unlike the case of its other categories, the IGFA is gender-blind when it comes to fly tackle. That's why I had to call the IGFA to determine whether the current twelve-pound-test-tippet record holder, Beryl E. Bliss—with a striper of sixty-four pounds, eight ounces—is a man or a woman. (He's a man.) The fish was caught in the Smith River[2]—not far up the Oregon coast from where Joe caught his Coos Bay fish. Sadly, although four of the seven fly-rod-record striped bass were caught on the West Coast, three of those four records are more than twenty years old and not likely ever to be topped by other Pacific Coast fish.

---

[1]Outdoor writer Joseph D. Bates Jr. is best remembered for his book on *Atlantic Salmon Flies and Fishing* (1970). However, many contemporaries knew him best for popularizing *Spinning for Salt Water Game Fish* (1957).

[2]The Smith and Umpqua Rivers are tributaries of the same estuary.

The best of what's left of striped bass fishing in the West is found in and around San Francisco Bay. But then the greatest number of stripers has always been found there. In 1905, when Louis Rhead published *The Basses Fresh-Water and Marine*,[3] contributor Dr. Tarleton H. Bean noted that "the [striped] bass have not gone far north or south of the Golden Gate. Russian River in Sonoma County seems to be almost the northern limit, while Monterey Bay is the southern boundary."

According to Dr. Bean, California state fish commissioners had a theory that "bass dislike to migrate far through salt water in order to reach other fresh-water streams." That's why, in December 1903, seventy-five bass "ranging from six ounces to three and a half pounds in weight" were shipped seven hundred miles south from San Francisco and planted in the Santa Aña River and San Diego Bay. Nothing came of the experiment, probably because theoretical salinity barriers have less to do with limiting the striper's range than a lack of suitable estuaries.

With hindsight, we now know it was only through the most wonderful luck that the first striped bass shipments were sent to the most compatible location for this species anywhere along the Pacific Coast. In the Asbury Park Fishing Club yearbook for 1924, A. H. McCloud reported that "the first planting shipment [in 1879] consisted of some 130 fish, ranging from one and one-half to five inches in length, and about 30 medium-sized fish." These stripers were seined and

[3]Bookseller Judith Bowman describes this book as "a masterpiece of artistic binding, bound to resemble a [striped] bass with painted scales on the covers, fins on the spine—the book is so beautiful, no wonder the dust jacket is so rare."

shipped from New Jersey's Navesink-Shrewsbury ecosystem not many miles north of where the Asbury Park Fishing Club was founded a decade later.

"A few of these died enroute," McCloud said, "and the remaining of the lot were deposited in the Straits of Carquinez at Martinez, California.

"During the month of June, 1882, a second lot of 450 fish were collected from the Shrewsbury river, New Jersey, and the shipment arrived in California during the latter part of July. Of these 450 fish, a little more than 300 of them came through in good condition and were planted in Suisun bay at Army Point, near Suisun."

Although stripers stocked in California eventually strayed to Oregon, it's interesting to speculate whether a regular annual coastal migration, comparable to the one between the Chesapeake and New England, would have developed had a different gene pool been used to populate the West. Hudson River fish, like those in the Navesink-Shrewsbury ecosystem, frequently migrate to Maine, but some Chesapeake stripers regularly make it all the way to Nova Scotia. Salmon of the same species, but born in different rivers, have different migration patterns encoded in their DNA. Why not different stocks of striped bass?

Even without wanderlust genes, however, the transplanted stripers flourished in the San Francisco Bay watershed. By 1949—according to an estimate by Dr. Alex Calhoun of the California Department of Fish and Game and reported by Leon Adams—some "243,000 men, women and children, in the course of two million man-days of legal sport fishing [that year], caught approximately 1,750,000 striped bass. That means an average catch of almost one striped bass per man-day of fishing. The average successful angler takes 18 to 25 bass per year. (Fortunately for the cause of conservation, 32 percent of the fishermen don't catch any.) The average party-boat passenger takes one bass per half-day trip. The average weight per striped bass caught is about four pounds."

These numbers may be high. Dr. Calhoun extrapolated his data from a postseason postcard survey. In the early 1970s, the California Department of Fish and Game began comparing anglers' estimates with their actual catches and found that fishermen look back on the previous season through extremely rosy-tinted glasses, indeed—reporting approximately 6.5 times as many fish as they actually catch. On the other hand, a relatively small number of dedicated anglers were killing hundreds of stripers each year but keeping that information to themselves, particularly as the species declined in the '70s. The length to which such anglers would go to keep their catches secret was described in "Midnight Stripers" by Russell Chatham in the March 1977 issue of *Field & Stream*. Chatham and his fishing partner preferred letting a couple of cops think they'd been smoking pot—"one joint was it"—rather than fishing at night (illegal at the time), or allowing the police to look in the trunk of Chatham's car and find six stripers stashed there—all taken on a fly and all weighing between fifteen and twenty-five pounds.

California pioneered striped bass conservation when in 1915—decades before the first size or daily restrictions appeared in the East—the state declared striped bass to be *game-fish* and limited sportfishermen to five fish per day, none of which could be less than twelve inches in length. Over time, the daily limit shrank and the minimum size increased. By the early 1960s, anglers could keep only three fish per day at least sixteen inches long. Today, the daily limit is two fish at least eighteen inches long. Unfortunately, these rules have done little to prevent the striper's decline. Unlike the case of the East, where overfishing is the primary reason for the periodic collapse of striper stocks, in California it's power and water projects and the thirst of too many millions of Californians who think little about the ecological repercussions of their merely being there that have all but finished Pacific stripers.

In 1949, California pioneered a point system for striped bass management that was later adopted by the federal government for waterfowl. An angler could keep five striped bass a day, but not in excess of a formula of twenty-five pounds, plus one fish. As Leon Adams tried to explain the system: "If four six-pounders and a fifty-pounder were caught in that order, they would be within the weight limit; but a twelve-pounder, a thirteen-pounder, and a two-pounder, caught in that order, would be a weight limit consisting of only three fish. There was an additional proviso that regardless of weight, an angler could keep at least two fish."

The point system for striped bass failed for the same reason the federal point system later failed for waterfowl: It was too complicated. The average person didn't understand it, and when he did, he reordered the sequence of his catches to keep the most possible fish.

In 1969, the California Department of Fish and Game decided to inventory all coastal stripers. It came up with an estimate of 1.6 million adult fish. Three years later, the assessment peaked at 1.9 million. From then on, it has steadily declined. In 1993, the total number of adult stripers was thought to be just 765,000 fish, of which an estimated 200,000 came from hatcheries. This latter contribution has ended, thanks to the National Marine Fisheries Service's proscription of Pacific coastal stripers. "Mitigation fish," provided and paid for by industrial water-users, are now released exclusively in inland reservoirs.

"Striped bass fishing is a relict sport in California," says Don Stevens. "It's still hot when stripers are found feeding off a beach, or a charter skipper spots a school on his fish-finder. But the charter fleet mostly sails for potluck today. Rockfish [not striped bass, but members of a family of Pacific fish, the Scorpaenidae] are always dependable, and in recent years we've had a bonanza of California halibut. But few anglers catch two stripers a year anymore—much less their legal limit of two a day."

Fortunately for Don, Russell Chatham, and me, we still have memories of San Francisco Bay during the Last Hurrah of striper angling there in the 1960s.

# · 7 ·

# CALIFORNIA DREAMING

PACIFIC COAST ANGLERS have often experimented and inno-
vated more than their tradition-bound Atlantic cousins. Off
the East Coast, for example, lures are still trolled near bottom
the way they've always been: with heavy in-line or three-way-
swivel-attached sinkers. Whatever weights Atlantic anglers put
on their lines, they expect back. By contrast, Pacific anglers
were among the first to experiment with weighted lines. Monel
and braided-wire lines were developed in the 1950s. When
these weren't enough to take spoons or jigs to the bottom,
West Coast anglers came up with a sinker release that held
two or three pounds of cumbersome weight, but dropped
the load when a fish hit. This ingenious device was comprised of 2½ inches of ⅜-inch copper tubing, crimped or
sealed with brass swivels and eyes at either end, and a spring

mechanism inside the tube that released the weight whenever something tugged on the leader.

The trouble was almost anything could trigger the release: a missed strike, a temporary snag, even a large jellyfish. At an average cost of $1 for three iron balls, an angler could go through quite a few bucks before he caught a limit of striped bass. Throughout the 1960s, so many tons of iron balls were dropped in San Francisco Bay that wags speculated an entrepreneur with a powerful magnet could recover enough scrap to rebuild our nation's merchant marine fleet. By the end of that decade, however, Great Lakes anglers had taken the release concept and reversed it so that the line, and not the weight, pulled free on a strike. Thus, the downrigger was born to catch salmon introduced to the Midwest from the Pacific, just as the sinker release had been developed to catch striped bass introduced to the Pacific from the Atlantic.

Not all San Francisco anglers were receptive to such new ideas. Some weren't even receptive to a transplanted species such as the striper. Russell Chatham recalled one member of the Golden Gate Angling and Casting Club who regularly declared, "The only thing lower than a striped bass fisherman is a deer hunter!" Yet the club also had members such as Chatham and outdoor columnist Jules Cuerin, who—one summer day in 1925—became the first fly fisherman known to catch striped bass in Pacific waters. He caught a pair of twenty-five-pounders while casting from the deck of a party boat in San Francisco Bay.

Several members were also innovative in being the first anglers in the nation to experiment with shooting heads and lead-core fly lines. Some of the techniques that Russell Chatham recommended in *Striped Bass on the Fly* (1977) he learned at the club. However, he learned many more on his own. Russell David Chatham was born in San Francisco on October 27, 1939. He grew up in the Bay Area teaching himself to paint, write, and fly fish while working as a sign painter, printer, carpenter, journalist, cabinetmaker, illustrator, and college instructor. In 1950, Chatham recalled, an uncle showed him "a Gibbs striper fly. . . . Its delicate composition of bucktail and teal breast plainly mocked such tackle box standbys as the pyramid sinker and snelled hook. I had always liked to fish for stripers anyway, but now I could see the sun rising above a bright new horizon."

Nonetheless, Chatham went on using bait and spinning tackle until a series of incidents convinced him it was "a mistake to assume that by using a fly you are handicapping yourself. If you can control your equipment and learn when and where to fish, you have precisely the same chance as with any other type of tackle. In fact . . . what the flycaster lacks in casting distance and perhaps depth [compared with anglers who use conventional casting or spinning tackle], he makes up for with an extended knowledge of habitat and habits."

Some fly casters, anyway. Listen to how Chatham cut through the nonsense of trying to "match the hatch" in saltwater fishing. "Among knowledgeable fishermen, it is said that if you still think fly patterns matter, you haven't fished enough.

. . . Black and white, large and small is pretty much the long and short of it. My experience has led me to believe that when they are biting at all, they will bite at almost anything. Striped bass are not tackle wise, nor are they wise at all. They are simply instinctive creatures who survive by reflexes in a domain of gloomy light and turbulent currents. Inventing a new fly pattern for them is about as important as inventing an elevator that goes sideways."

Governmental biologists, who may fish only a few times a year, underestimate the impact of devotees who fish every spare moment they have. A single hardcore angler can make a serious dent in a population of adult fish, as Chatham himself acknowledged. Not long after high school, he "met a man named Walt Mullen who liked to plug cast for bass. He used to fish around the ferry slip at Point San Quentin and kept right on doing it while the Richmond–San Rafael Bridge was being built. One morning, about the time the bridge was opened for business, Walt took me out. When we arrived back at the dock two hours later, my life was ruined. In the next ten years I caught no less than five thousand bass at that one spot alone"—including the thirty-six-pounder that broke Joe Brooks's record.

Chatham caught that fish more than halfway through my first tour in Vietnam, a tour that figuratively began when I quit Columbia's graduate program in English and comparative literature and moved to Berkeley, California. President Kennedy's New Frontier was still in vogue, and I sought some greater meaning to life than what I'd found in seminars on medieval drama. I'd left secondary school teaching and law school for much the same reason: I didn't want the world to think they were all I could do. I harbored a fear—less of failure than of success, which may be a syndrome peculiar to children of successful fathers.

I lived in a one-room apartment over a garage on Channing Way. I was there to deal with my desire not so much to write a novel as to have written one. An already published friend insisted I start with an outline. So I made endless outlines and kept notes in ever-growing piles, first on my desk, then on the floor, finally even by the tub and toilet. Preparation and organization became substitutes for writing itself.

Meanwhile, my landlord wanted his rent. Without considering more conventional options, I began freelancing fishing and travel articles. After the first checks arrived, writing fiction seemed less relevant. Unfortunately, small magazines more often pay on publication than on acceptance. That meant that while I usually had enough for the rent, I had little to spare for such essential luxuries as my weekly party-boat fishing trip from the Berkeley docks.

Even today I can't see a picture of the Golden Gate Bridge without recalling the many large stripers I caught in the shadow of its South Tower. The long reach of Raccoon Straits between Tiburon and Angel Island might mean sailing to some, but to me it meant drifting, casting, jigging, and occasionally catching a striped bass. At Alcatraz, whenever the party boat "swung the rock" to hook one of the big fish holding close to shore, prison guards bellowed at us through bullhorns.

By August 1964, I was owed several thousand dollars for unpublished pieces but had less than $40 in my pocket. Since boot camp was a nearly universal bonding experience for draft-aged males of my generation, and since I was twenty-five and would soon be exempt, why not join the navy? A recruiter in San Francisco allowed as how Uncle Sam would not only advance me enough money to pay off my debts, he'd also send me all the way back east to officer candidates' school in Rhode Island. So I signed some papers, raised my right hand, and swore allegiance to the Constitution. I timed my enrollment date for the autumn striper run in Newport.

At dawn on April Fool's Day, 1966—a few months before Chatham caught his world-record striper—I was blown up in my hotel in the Chinese district of Saigon. I was on the top floor, which didn't collapse, so my injuries were minor. My Australian colleagues, who'd always thought they were lucky to sleep on the ground floor so they didn't have to climb the steps whenever the elevator wasn't working—which was often—were killed.

By July 1968, I'd completed two tours in Vietnam and was back in the States teaching at the U.S. Naval Academy when the first of my California striped bass stories, "The Stripers of Alcatraz," appeared in *Fishing World* magazine. I received payment for it just as I set off for a tour as an interpreter-translator at the Paris Peace Talks. My last San Francisco Bay story was published in the May/June 1970 issue of the same magazine, by which time I'd left the navy and the Paris negotiations

in protest over what I considered to be an unnecessary delay in
ending an unwinnable war.

No one likes to think he has wasted any part of his life.
Writers are luckier than most in being able to use almost all
of our experiences as grist for the creative mill. Yet, except
for a couple of technical essays for the *Foreign Service Journal*
and the *Proceedings* of the Naval Institute, I've never published anything about what I did or saw in Vietnam or at the
Paris Peace Talks. At first, I was prohibited by certain secrecy
documents I'd signed. Later, it was because editors would accept only orthodox truths about the war. Now it's a matter of
my being typecast. The pigeonholing process, which I sought
to escape by ducking the Ph.D., caught up with me anyway
since I'm now categorized as an outdoor writer, and what
could a hooks-and-bullets hack possibly have to say about
Vietnam?

In looking back on my California days, I'm struck by
how completely I missed seeing the handwriting on the
wall for striped bass. Like almost everyone else—except
Leon Adams—I thought the good times would roll on forever. I didn't even realize how inferior the 1960s were in
comparison with earlier decades. Yet, writing in 1953,
Adams noted that "poachers fishing illegally have depleted
the bass population by an undetermined figure, preying
mostly on larger spawning fish favored by the restaurant
bootleg trade. Every year additional thousands of stripers
have been trapped and suffocated in irrigation ditches, or

churned into fish-burger by industrial pumping plants, poisoned by insecticides, other chemicals, and sewage, or eaten alive by sea lions."

The 1930s were Adams's golden years when, despite the Great Depression, the quality of life for a Californian who valued good wine and simple recreation over excess and luxury was at its peak. He pinned the tail squarely on the donkey's rump when he wrote, "The threats to the striper population result basically from human population growth. During the 1940's one of the greatest human migrations in history took place. Swarms of people moved westward, overflowed the Pacific Coast cities, spawned new industries, built new towns along the waterways, multiplied the pollution of inland waters, and added hordes of anglers to those already killing striped bass. Meanwhile, ever-increasing rivers of water were being pumped out of the bass-spawning and nursery grounds to irrigate the fertile central valley; and untold numbers of the baby fish were sucked up with the water, to die in the pumps or in the canals beyond."

The great fishing that Russell Chatham imbibed—and I, too, briefly tasted—in the decade following the publication of Adams's book was a glorious sunset for an already moribund sport. Accelerating that decline was the advent of the live-bait industry. Prior to 1962, most party-boat fishing for San Francisco stripers was done by trolling. Even the use of hefty weights and sinker releases meant that trolling captains were limited to parties of six or seven anglers. By contrast, live-bait boats accommodate two or three times that number of clients and thus had two to three times the impact on stripers. Deep trolling with large lures was still the most effective way to take trophy fish, but I was surprised by how many twenty- and even thirty-pound striped bass my headboat companions and I caught while drifting live anchovies—so long as the baits were fished deep.

In 1962, there were fewer than a dozen live-bait boats in the Bay Area. By 1963, forty San Francisco charter boats were equipped with large live wells. By 1964, the total was nearly one hundred. Whenever a skipper found a school of stripers, he'd radio friends, who'd rush to the scene with dozens of other boats following. As soon as all the anglers aboard had their limits of three fish each, the skippers rushed back to port, hoping to corral another party of anglers for the afternoon tide.

One of the ironies of Russell Chatham's guide to striped bass fly fishing is that it was published seven years after Chatham had abandoned the Bay Area for the less crowded waters of Montana. According to a 1994 survey, there're now more than 467,000 marine anglers in northern California, and 1.15 million in the entire state. Yet, according to a 1993 survey, there're barely 765,000 adult striped bass left along coastal California, including the 200,000 hatchery fish that won't be there in the future.

With those kinds of numbers, how can state biologists continue to condone a daily limit of two stripers per licensed angler? Recreational fishing rules should be designed to enhance quality angling, not terminal yield. They also shouldn't be set according to politically correct notions of fairness. It's ironic that the state that once led the nation in innovative rules for perpetuating local striper populations, and new techniques for catching the fish, should now be superintending their demise.

# ·8·

# THE SAVANNAH RIVER

WILLIAM ELLIOTT WAS a rare man of his time. A successful South Carolina rice planter, he was also a devout Unionist—perhaps a result of his education at Harvard College. Elliot forecast dire consequences if his hothead neighbors forced secession in the South, and he lived just long enough (1788–1863) to see his worst-case predictions come true.

In happier times—in 1846, to be precise—he published a book about hunting and fishing in coastal Carolina. Since he knew that many readers would be Yankees, he was careful to distinguish southern and northern races of striped bass by noting that "this fish, in very fine condition is taken at the South in *fresh water* [Elliott's emphasis] rivers." However, he may have misled some readers who didn't realize that the Carolina Low Country is so very low, many rivers that flow fresh on outgoing tides flow salt, or at least brackish, on incoming tides for dozens of miles up from the sea. Stripers are caught on their spawning runs as far upstream as they can swim, which—in the days before the U.S. Army Corps of Engineers so extensively dammed the region—meant well into the interior realm of catfish and crappies. Thus, whereas northern stripers normally migrate north and south along the coast, southern stripers are more inclined to move east and west within the same riverine ecosystem.

Whenever I tell angling friends that I've caught striped bass in every state along the Atlantic Coast from Maine to Georgia (except New Hampshire), I get the same funny look. If my friends are New Englanders, they can't quite imagine a coastal striped bass fishery south of the Chesapeake. Even some of my southern friends are surprised to learn they have notable "rockfishing" anywhere other than in landlocked lakes.

Not long after a story of mine about fishing the Savannah River appeared in the November 1972 issue of *Field & Stream,* I attended a southern outdoor writers' conference in South Carolina, where I heard two colleagues discussing my article in the bus seat behind me. They evidently didn't believe that stripers existed in the river separating our host state from Georgia. One suggested that the picture accompanying the story, of angler Jack Wegner with a forty-pound striper, was "faked," and the story itself, "a crock." I was aggravated and almost butted in. Then I regretted even writing the article, for the fewer who know about the Savannah, the better.

There's no river quite like it. One moment you're catching channel bass and black drum in South Carolina. The next you're taking striped bass and seatrout in Georgia. If your cast is long enough, you could catch all four species in both states without moving your boat.

When the action slows down, you wait for a freighter or a shrimp boat. No special freighter or shrimp boat—just something big enough to roll out a surflike wake to wash down the banks and rouse the fish to feed again.

Or you wait for the tide to change. There's nothing half-day about this. It seems to occur about once an hour. Or even more. Through some mysterious workings of the river, one minute you're anchored fore and aft in an eddy catching stripers in a rip behind the boat. The next minute—and all without moving—the tide is boiling alongside, and you're hard put to keep your bait or lure near bottom. But before you can pull your anchor to find a new spot, the "tide" turns again and you see stripers swirling in a new rip off the bow. You're suddenly fishing 180 degrees from where you were fifteen minutes before. And all without moving the boat. Your surroundings seem changed, and if you weren't anchored, or if you'd never fished the Savannah River before, you'd think you were going nuts.

My wife was used to it; I was not. She was born and raised in Savannah; I'm just a boy from Brooklyn and Queens. When we fished the river, nothing seemed a surprise to Barbara. Everything did to me. And pleasantly so.

I'd gone to Savannah to write an exposé of an American Cyanamid facility generating—*and dumping directly into the river*—more than twelve thousand tons a week of sulfuric acid, ferrous sulfate, and other liquid wastes. Under pressure by the state to stop the dumping, the plant manager had concocted a scheme to transport the poisonous stuff offshore and dump it in the Gulf Stream instead. My pitch was, why dump it at all? Sulfuric acid is a valuable compound that could be recycled to create jobs, not destroy marine life. After my story, "The Great Acid Dump," appeared in the December 1972 issue of *Field & Stream,* American Cyanamid decided to recycle and did, indeed, create new jobs.

In the meanwhile, I'd been intrigued by the "smell test" used by local Georgians to gauge the edibility of Savannah-caught fish: If a striper has an industrial odor when it's landed, it's released. If a kept fish smells like petroleum when it's gutted, it goes on the compost heap. If the fish still smells like a fish after it's cleaned, they'll be rockfish fillets and collards for dinner—although I still wondered about those unseen side orders of mercury and lead.

Despite all the abuse funneled her way, the Savannah is a beautiful waterway to fish. Her many cuts and channels curl and flow through high-grassed banks lined by live oaks and cabbage palms. Anglers have a soul-satisfying outing, whether they catch fish they can eat or not. After a heavy rain, the water runs brown or yellow from erosion, but that's typical of most southern streams and has nothing to do with industrial waste. Indeed, some soil nutrients carried downstream contribute to the care and breeding of the myriad shrimp and menhaden that make up the bulk of the stripers' diet.

Baxter McCreery, a civil engineer with the Army Corps of Engineers, was Barbara's and my host for our morning of fishing. Saltwater-angling writer Milt Rosko also came along. A lifelong New Jerseyite, Milt was skeptical of the very idea of coastal stripers south of Delaware Bay. He certainly wasn't prepared to swallow the tales Baxter greeted us with as we loaded his boat.

"My best day last season, I caught a dozen stripers ranging up to forty-two pounds. The smallest weighed twenty-five."

"Twenty-five pounds was your small one, eh?" asked Milt with a wink my way.

"Oh, we regularly get fish up to forty pounds in January when the run picks up," said Baxter. "Largest one I ever caught was only forty-four, but a friend has gotten two forty-eight-pounders. We're sure there're fifty-pound fish in the river."

It was getting a bit deep for me, too. Yet Baxter's tales were later confirmed by Bob Rees of the Richmond Hill Hatchery when I called to ask about its striper stocking program. Rees allowed as how most of the male fish he took from the Savannah were small—two pounds average, to a maximum of twenty-seven pounds—but the females were generally larger. "The cows regularly reach thirty-five pounds, and we occasionally see them over fifty."

Stripers start moving up the Savannah in October as the river cools. Angling for the smaller, mostly male fish is good through early December when the larger females start to show up. The best fishing is from just before Christmas through January and into February, though Baxter has caught fish well into March. By this late date, however, the most enterprising striped bass have run the nearly two hundred miles upstream past Augusta as far as the Clark Hill Reservoir dam, spawned, and are on their way back again. Baxter is convinced local anglers are missing a beat by not fishing for the returnees: "In February, most everyone is fishing for seatrout, but there're big rockfish in the river all spring long."

Rees said he has taken big stripers with his shocking equipment even in May. "There're some in the river all year round, but we're not interested in them once they've spawned."

"What do you do with the fingerlings from your hatchery?" I asked.

"We send them all across the country—wherever they're needed to start a landlocked fishery."

Most Savannah stripers stay in the river-and-delta ecosystem year-round. Others use the river to spawn, but wander afterward. I've caught striped bass in South Carolina's portion of the Intracoastal Waterway where it's unlikely the fish are year-round residents. I imagine they use the brackish corridor the way boaters do: ranging north and south between connecting coastal bays and sounds.

"With this high tide, we'll try Field's Cut where it joins the north channel of the Savannah River," said Baxter. "Should be fish around the pilings."

When we arrived less than fifteen minutes after leaving the marina at Thunderbolt, I asked Baxter where the pilings were.

"They're just at the edge of the weeds," he said, pointing to an area of open water. "There was a plantation here before the Rebellion, and stumps are all that's left of a dock once used for loading rice. You'll see the tops at low tide if we stay here that long. But I suspect you'll have all the fish you want by ten o'clock."

Milt gave me another one of his skeptical looks, and we began rigging up. The lines on our borrowed reels were ten- to thirty-pound-test monofilament. While such tackle is obviously too heavy for the three-pound stripers we anticipated, Baxter said he liked being loaded for bear in case Big Momma showed up.

Terminal gear on the Savannah is typical of shoal-water tackle all along the Southeast Coast: a large, long balsa bobber cocked by an ounce of lead with a 2/0 hook. The preferred bait is live shrimp. In January, trolling with plugs is popular because, by then, shrimp are hard to obtain and harder still to keep active in the cold river water in the live wells.

Baxter swears by a red-and-white pattern for his plugs. He believes that above all other colors, or color combinations, striped bass like plugs with red heads and white bodies. Yet other Savannah fishermen swear by a blue-scaled "mullet" design. When I asked Baxter about the blue-scaled option, he conceded that some fish in the river appear to fancy blue plugs, but a majority of obviously more sensible rockfish still prefer red and white. Blue-plug aficionados believe the opposite, of course. What it boils down to—as always—is that you catch stripers on the lures you use, and because you catch stripers on those lures, you use them over all others, thereby ensuring that they become the "best" in your box.

To show us how to catch Savannah stripers, Baxter caught the first fish. Then I caught a small channel bass. Then Barbara caught a striper. Then Baxter. Then Barbara. The two of them took turns the rest of the morning catching most of the fish. Milt and I decided this was because Dixie stripers are more sympathetic to native-born Georgians.

I managed to catch up for a while after I picked up one of Baxter's plug-casting outfits equipped with a yellow bucktail. For fifteen minutes, I was top angler, as every striper in the river seemed to show a sudden liking for yellow bucktail. I caught four fish of up to seven pounds in quick succession. Suddenly, sadly, they refused to give me another nudge. Either I'd caught all the fish in the vicinity turned on by yellow, or word had gotten out that my yelps of joy were decidedly un-Rebel-like. There being no other artificial lure aboard, I went back to live shrimp.

Meanwhile, Milt countered with his own brand of savvy. A widely acknowledged authority on flounder and flattie fishing, Milt confirmed his reputation by catching a southern fluke. My teasing him was a little unfair since, in 1966, he'd written a popular book on the *Secrets of Striped Bass Fishing*. In addition, when the action slowed for everyone else, Milt kept us supplied with sea catfish. Finally, after lulling the suspicions of the local stripers with his Jersey tactics, Milt caught the largest of the day—an eight-pounder, hooked on the bottom on a very dead shrimp.

"We have some kind of fishing in the river all year long," said Baxter, "but the best time is winter. You come out at dawn, shoot a limit of mallards or bluebills, and then spend the remainder of the morning trolling for big rockfish."

"Do you eat all you keep?" Milt asked, eyeing the growing number of fish in the cooler.

"These rocks are small and new to the river. By January and February, after the fish have been here a while, we release most of what we catch. And unless they're exceptionally large, we release all the big ones because they're loaded with roe."

And probably with toxins, too, I thought.

"I hope you'll take some of the fish," urged Baxter. So Barbara and I packed several in ice and flew with them that afternoon to her father's home in Atlanta. At dinner, and despite some anxiety, everyone agreed that early-run Savannah stripers passed all the appropriate taste tests.

Although my father-in-law died a number of years ago, I had a hunch Baxter McCreery might still be in the phone book. He answered on the second ring.

"Yes, I'm still fishing the Savannah," he said, "though less today in retirement than when I had only weekends to fish. When I worked eight to four, five days a week, I fished every Saturday and Sunday, rain or shine. Now that I can go out any time I like, I go out less often. Funny about that. Maybe I just need to fish less today. But the catching is a whole lot less, too."

Anglers are no longer allowed to keep striped bass from the Savannah River. It's not because of contamination, but because of scarcity. After insisting for decades that Savannah fish comprised a local population unaffected by coastal trends, biologists now blame the decline of Georgia stripers on the same alleged cyclical influences that supposedly caused the collapse of striped bass stocks all along the Atlantic seaboard. The hitch in this theory is that, while striper populations from North Carolina to New England have rebounded since the late 1980s, Savannah stripers have not. Furthermore, no one in authority is willing to connect the decline of Georgia stripers to the fact that shrimp trawling in the region has escalated enormously over the past two decades.

McCreery knows several biologists and likes them personally. That may be why he's so unwilling to question their assumptions. He knows how much harder all fishermen must work today to catch a fraction as many fish, but he gives the biologists the benefit of the doubt and parrots their theory that stripers are subject to cycles, "like foxes and rabbits." When I point out that modern netters can outfish all the sea's "foxes" combined, Baxter concedes there may be a connection between intensified shrimping in local bays and sounds and the decrease of most local marine fish, including striped bass. But almost immediately, he adds that not much can be done to manage such a "cyclical species" as the rockfish.

When I ask Baxter whether he ever goes back to the Field's Cut pilings where we fished a quarter century ago, he says, no, because they're on the South Carolina side of the river, and he hasn't bothered to buy a South Carolina tidal license.

"Is there anything better about fishing the Savannah to-day?" I ask.

Baxter is silent a moment. "Well, when you were here, you either had to know somebody with a boat or bring your own to get on the water. Today, we have a local guides' association whose members pick you up at your hotel and return you after fishing."

That's progress, I suppose. Fewer fish, but more convenience, even when that convenience may be another reason there're fewer fish.

My conversation with Baxter reinforced my conviction that I did the right thing in becoming a freelance writer when I did. Unlike my father, who decided to make money first and enjoy life later, then found that much of what he most enjoyed about life was no longer there, I elected to follow my bliss first and worry about making money later. Freelancing enabled me to do the former even as I continue to worry about the latter. Still, over the past quarter century, I've skimmed the cream of angling from Alaska to Zululand and enjoyed a thousand more dawns and evenings on the water than I would have known in any other line of work. I have no regrets for the roads not taken, but I do feel sad about the many fine places I've fished that no longer offer quality angling.

The Savannah River's pollution is now under control, but its rockfishing is a matter of memory. From an engineering point of view, the river's improved. From an angling point of view, the river's dying. Why can't the two be compatible?

# THE ROANOKE RIVER

THE AGE OF angling superstars is drawing to a close. Forty years ago, Joe Brooks, A. J. McClane, and Lee Wulff were familiar names to anyone with a subscription to *Field & Stream, Outdoor Life,* or *Sports Afield.* These magazines were the sportsmen's equivalent of Metro-Goldwyn-Mayer and Universal Studios. They both popularized and glamorized angling—especially fly angling—and the people who regularly wrote about it. Brooks, McClane, and Wulff designed or introduced new rods, reels, lines, and flies, and pioneered places that have since become mandatory stops on every affluent angler's Grand Tour.

Today, the Hollywood studio system has fractured into dozens of smaller production companies. Likewise, the outdoor press has many more highly specialized magazines competing for the angler's attention. Modern stars shine less brightly than did Brooks, Wulff, and McClane because they must shed their light across so many more venues. Even so, a few are so prolific that their omnipresence has made them known to anglers everywhere.

One of these is a septuagenarian (he likes it when you talk dirty) who created a streamer pattern featured on a stamp. On May 31, 1991, the U.S. Postal Service issued five "Fishing Flies" (29-cent) stamps designed by wildlife artist Chuck Ripper. The series was intended to commemorate American fly fishing. However, in addition to Canadian Don Gapen's Muddler Minnow—an understandable mistake since Americans have always laid claim to anything interesting coming out of Canada—the series included the Jock Scott, a salmon fly created by a ghillie of that name and first used in Scotland about 1850. The Mickey Finn would have been equally colorful and uniquely American, but a senior postal service bureaucrat thought the name had criminal connotations—which, of course, it does. The final series included Lee Wulff's Royal Wulff, Stu Apte's Tarpon Fly, and Lefty Kreh's Lefty's Deceiver.

Bernard Victor Kreh—alias Lefty, as in the streamer he designed circa 1958 for striped bass fishing in the Chesapeake—was born on February 16, 1925, in Frederick, Maryland. Although he has roamed the world since, Lefty remains a Marylander at heart and still lives in that state—albeit in more upscale circumstances than he knew as a boy when he supplemented his widowed mother's meager income by bush-bobbing for catfish and trapping muskrat and mink. Not only did such experiences imprint Lefty with a love of nature, they gave him the common touch—that special gift of all good educators and politicians. However, this particular Pied Piper uses a fly rod rather than a flute to fascinate kids of all ages. Over the quarter century I've known Lefty, I've invariably found him in the middle of a crowd—whether it was hundreds at a National Wildlife Federation "Summit" or just a dozen in a diner. Looking back, I can recall only once when I had Lefty to myself (and another friend) for a morning of fishing near my home on the Eastern Shore of Virginia. Otherwise, I merely wave to him over the heads of fans surrounding him at conventions and angling clinics.

That's why I jumped at the chance to fish with him in the spring of 1995. Our host—C. H. "Chuck" Laughridge III—wanted Lefty, Tom Earnhardt (also an angling author), and me to fish North Carolina's Roanoke River after the close of the regular striped bass season. Stripers are still abundant in the upper reaches of the river, but most local fishermen stay home if they can't keep what they catch. I'd fished with Chuck the previous year and left my tackle at home. So I'd borrowed one of Chuck's light bait-casting rods, flipped his quarter-ounce jigs, and caught and released more than fifty striped bass averaging three to six pounds in four phenomenally fast fishing hours. I looked forward to seeing what we could do with our fly rods.

The striper's recent recovery has been more dramatic in the Roanoke–Albemarle Sound watershed than any other estuarine system along the Atlantic Coast. Indeed, Roanoke stripers have recovered to the point that Weldon, North Carolina—which as far back as the 1940s billed itself as the "Rockfish Capital"—broadened its sobriquet in '93 so that motorists on Interstate 95 would know they were passing by the "Striped Bass Capital of the World." Twenty years ago, no one in that sleepy hollow would have dreamed of making such a boast. Overfishing in the '70s and the uncertain release of water from dams above the prime spawning grounds had effectively closed the watershed's striper fishery. Many eastern Carolinians took the decline for granted. They'd endured boom-and-bust cycles since the 1830s when a canal and a railroad first put the region on interstate maps. By 1840, the 160-plus-mile stretch of rail line between Wilmington and Weldon—already being extended into Virginia—was advertised as the longest railway on earth. During the Civil War, it was the vital link connecting Richmond to the only Confederate port that blockade-runners were able to slip into and out of with some impunity.

As was true elsewhere in the South, the postwar decades were hard. By 1891, however, local businessmen had begun constructing what was to be the largest cotton mill in the state, established a winery near the old Roanoke Canal aqueduct, and circulated a brochure suggesting that Weldon's potential for hydropower was second only to Minneapolis in the entire United States. That same year, at the confluence of the Roanoke, Cashie, and Chowan Rivers in Batchelor Bay, the largest striped bass ever recorded was taken in a net and brought to Edenton for sale. She weighed 125 pounds. Sixty-one years later, novelist Win Brooks paid homage to this fish by having his giant striper-heroine in *The Shining Tides* spawn in "the milt-chalked Roanoke above Albemarle Sound."

The region's upbeat economy began to stumble around the turn of the century, along with its overfished population of striped bass. In 1909, the Garrett Winery—the last major employer in Weldon—moved to Virginia because of North Carolina's new prohibition laws. The Roanoke Navigation and Power Company, which had used the fall of water from the old canal's aqueduct to generate power for local industries, was on the brink of bankruptcy. On the eve of World War I, the only tourists in Weldon were sons and daughters of Confederate sick and wounded who'd been shipped south from Virginia battlefields, died, and been buried in the makeshift cemetery in the woods by the rail line.

The Depression seemed to come sooner and last longer in eastern Carolina than in the rest of the nation. World War II didn't change things much, except to siphon off another generation of young farmers and send them to battlefields in Europe and the Pacific. The next economic upswing didn't begin until 1953, when the John H. Kerr dam was completed on the Roanoke, flooding 37,500 acres in Virginia (where the project is known as the Bugg's[1] Island dam and lake) and 12,500 acres

[1] Rightly speaking, the project should be named neither for Samuel Bugg, the first English settler, nor for John H. Kerr, the North Carolina congressman who got the project funded, but for the Occoneechee tribe of Native Americans who lived in the area from at least 1250 to 1676, when they were wiped out by Nathaniel Bacon and his followers.

in North Carolina. This was followed in 1955 by the Roanoke Rapids dam, and in 1963 by the Gaston dam. A significant portion of the entire river is now locked into a chain of lakes sprawling from near my mother's birthplace in South Boston, Virginia, to Weldon, more than seventy-five crow-flight miles downstream. Altogether, the lakes created more than twelve hundred miles of shoreline and encompass over fifteen thousand square miles of watershed.

By the late 1960s, the value of the reservoirs' recreation already exceeded the dams' hydroelectric and flood-control benefits. Power once generated for textile, paper-, and fiberboard mills went to the growing number of vacation and retirement homes. Developers were assured by the U.S. Army Corps of Engineers that they could build close to the lakes because "surplus water" could always be drained quickly downstream. Thus, the real-estate boom that had eluded local entrepreneurs in the nineteenth century finally swept through the Roanoke Valley in the 1970s.

But that boom had hidden costs, one of which was the failure of the river's striped bass population due to overfishing by anglers on the spawning grounds and netters in Albemarle Sound. In addition, an interagency agreement between the corps, which maintains Kerr Reservoir; Virginia Electric and Power Company (VEPCO), which generates power at the Gaston and Roanoke Rapids dams; and the North Carolina Wildlife Resources Commission (NCWRC), which wants water releases regulated for the benefit of fish and wildlife as well as power consumers, failed in 1971.

Although most newcomers bought their lakeside homes for the view, many also came for the area's reputedly excellent fishing. They supported the NCWRC in its effort to persuade the corps to consider downstream fisheries. The corps, however, regards itself more as a builder than a custodian. It thinks of dams and water exclusively in terms of flood control and power generation. Furthermore, it wasn't about to relinquish any of its authority to a state agency merely for the sake of fish.

This bureaucratic stalemate continued—and striper spawning languished—for the next seventeen years. Finally, in 1988—and due largely to heightened national (meaning congressional) concern for the striped bass—the corps promised a new multiagency group called the Roanoke River Water Flow Committee to reduce variability of water releases and to consult state biologists before ordering any extraordinary drawdowns. The committee seemed to have persuaded the corps that attempting to fine-tune water releases on an hourly basis did little to prevent potential flooding or enhance flows for power generation. More stable flows benefit not only homeowners along the lakes, who don't like seeing their docks rise and fall on something like a tidal basis, but also spawning striped bass.

The committee prevailed, less for the common sense it espoused than because it made its proposal at about the time that representatives of Virginia Beach, Virginia, asked to build a one-hundred-mile pipeline to draw sixty million gallons a day from Lake Gaston to support that coastal city's unbridled growth. The pipeline will affect water quality down even to

Albemarle Sound, which already suffers from perennial summer alga blooms caused by insufficient flushing of its tributary
rivers. Downstream problems, however, didn't alarm the corps
and VEPCO nearly as much as the possibility of having to
share "their" water—and, hence, their *authority*—with previously uninvolved agencies from the Commonwealth of Virginia. Thus, the corps and VEPCO became more attentive to
the wishes of the North Carolina Wildlife Resources Commission, hoping to play its conservation card off that of Virginia's
developers.

In the long run, it hasn't worked. The armies of development are still far mightier than those of conservation—
something the corps has long known and benefited by.
Construction of the Lake Gaston pipeline will commence in
the summer of 1997. However, during the first six years that
the corps cooperated with the Roanoke River Water Flow
Committee, striped bass production rose to record levels in
1988, '89, and '93. Fishing in the river rebounded so fast that
by the spring of '93, two local sportsmen—Chuck Laughridge
and Billy Green—founded the Roanoke Valley Striped Bass
Coalition to foster "more respect for striped bass." The coalition is composed mostly of local businessmen who want to
promote catch-and-release fishing to attract more tourist-
anglers to the area. They'd also like to persuade the state to buy
out the downstream commercial fishermen's striper allotment
of one hundred thousand pounds annually and transfer it to
the recreational side of the ledger. At $1 a pound, they point
out, one hundred thousand pounds are barely enough to

support four families of fishermen. Wouldn't it be smarter economically to allot those striped bass to anglers—especially catch-and-release anglers, who raise the value of fish to dozens of dollars per pound each time the same striper is caught and released?

As a North Carolina native and environmental lawyer, Tom Earnhardt knew a good deal about the politics behind our visit, but Lefty knew only that he was there to catch fish. While we launched the boats—Chuck Laughridge's johnboat, in which Tom and Lefty would fish, and the bass boat of another coalition member, Jim Frazier, in which I'd fish—Lefty kept scanning the river for signs of rising bass. Just before we stepped into our respective hulls, he noticed that I had a red-and-yellow Deceiver at the end of my leader. He snipped it off and replaced it with a chartreuse Clouser Minnow.

"I appreciate the compliment," he said, "but you might as well start with something giving you the best odds. I don't know why striped bass are so crazy for the color these days, but 'if it ain't chartreuse, it ain't no use.'"

The Deceiver had been my first choice not only as a compliment, but also because it's a dependable producer. Lefty created the fly to resemble a baitfish, yet be easy to tie and cast without fouling the hook. Since the streamer is more an idea than a pattern, it can be tied in a variety of colors and quantities of bucktail to alter its appearance, retrieving depth, and speed. And since the Roanoke was cloudy with silt from recent rains, I thought a medium dark pattern would show up well in the murky water. On the other hand, I couldn't argue with the fact that stripers everywhere these days seem turned on by chartreuse. Chartreuse jigs, spoons, even plastic eels are the preferred lure for chartermen from Montauk to Maryland. I also learned long ago never to spurn the advice (or free flies) of an angling expert.

We motored the short distance upstream to where eddies welled and boiled below the rapids. Lefty and Tom were trying poppers while I went deep with the Clouser. While they worked out longer and longer lengths of line, I struggled to get my sinking line more than fifty feet from the boat. Ever the educator, Lefty asked Chuck to motor over so he, Lefty, could show me a couple tricks to improve my casting. Within ten minutes, I was laying out half again as much line as I had before. Chuck allowed as how he'd like a lesson, too, and Lefty pretended to get angry.

"Oh, I get it! You fellows invited me down here for a free casting seminar! Well, you've got to show me some fish first!"

After the sun rose over the trees and shrank the shadowed areas of the river to just what lay near or under its brushy borders, Tom and Lefty switched to streamers and began a steady pick of striped bass. Lefty accurately covered water most other fly fishermen would have had to ignore. Yet he periodically turned his back on the more productive lies next to the bank to fish toward the middle of the river to give Tom first crack at the overhangs and snags.

Jim Frazier anchored me above a choice hole in an otherwise shallow stretch. For easier casting, I switched to a floating line, and almost immediately, a fish loomed up and took the fly. The striper turned, caught the current, and raced off with half my backing. I worked the fish in, and off it went again, but this time only to the end of the fly line. A few minutes later, I had the fish alongside, slipped the barbless fly from its jaw, and watched it vanish with a flip of its tail. The day was still young, and many fish lay ahead, but already it was complete, thanks to that fish, the fellowship, the brilliant sunshine glowing through countless newly minted leaves, the watchful herons perched on limbs along the banks, and an osprey that followed and fished with us for more than a mile downstream. It was an outing utterly devoid of competition or envy.

Biologists may have such feelings, but something in their training prevents them from seeing a river with the unalloyed enthusiasm of the amateur. The situation is analogous to what Mark Twain learned after he became a qualified riverboat skipper: "Now when I . . . had come to know every trifling feature that bordered the great river as familiarly as I knew the letters of the alphabet, I had made a valuable acquisition. But I had lost something, too. I had lost something which could never be restored to me while I lived. . . . The romance and beauty were all gone from the river. All the value any feature of it had for me now was the amount of usefulness it could furnish toward compassing the safe piloting of a steamboat. Since those days, I have pitied doctors from my heart. What does the lovely flush in a beauty's cheek mean to a doctor but a 'break' that ripples above some deadly disease? Are not all her visible charms sown thick with what are to him the signs and symbols of hidden decay? Does he ever see her beauty at all, or doesn't he simply view her professionally, and comment upon her unwholesome condition all to himself? And doesn't he sometimes wonder whether he has gained most or lost most by learning his trade?"

Fisheries biologists should be as much concerned with quality as quantity—with opportunity as well as pounds landed. The problem is that they're trained only to consider the landing side of the ledger, which is why they're preoccupied with maximum yield rather than optimum experience, and why catch-and-release anglers are penalized because the fish they release are ultimately assigned to somebody else's quota.

Most Roanoke River anglers want to improve the quality of their fishing. Most state biologists seem to care only about accumulating more data. If the data were being used to improve the quality of fishing, the anglers would put up with the frequent river shockings and other disruptions of their fishing opportunities. But the most obvious beneficiaries of data collecting are the biologists themselves, whose careers hinge on enhancing the maximum yield of the handful of commercial netters downstream—who, in turn, enjoy a four-to-one advantage over anglers in the state's allotment of striped bass. If the Roanoke system were made a recreational fishery only, the need for management would be reduced, and the river would attract tourist-anglers from all over the mid-Atlantic region. Yet whenever members of the Roanoke Valley Striped Bass Coalition raise that possibility with state officials, they're stonewalled.

"Making the striped bass a gamefish is elitist," say some politicians. "We must help the watermen," say others—which is like saying we must protect our dim commercial past from a bright recreational future. No wonder increasing numbers of anglers believe their state agencies no longer represent them. In 1995, public hearings were held in every coastal state from Maine to North Carolina to review state proposals to liberalize striped bass limits and seasons for recreational fishermen, and federal proposals to open up commercial netting for stripers beyond the states' three-mile limits. At every hearing, sport-fishermen voiced overwhelming opposition to liberalizing the regulations. Older anglers knew the striped bass weren't yet as fully recovered as the biologists claimed; even some commercial fishermen suggested it was prudent to let striper stocks continue to rebound. Yet the biocrats ignored the majority and did what they were planning to do all along. And everyone knew the reason: By providing more generous seasons and limits to the politically disorganized sportsmen, even more generous seasons and limits could be allotted to the politically adept netters.

In 1994, the now defunct Sport Fishing Institute listed its primary concerns as "dying habitats and deteriorating fisheries, managing waters for reasons other than fishing, encroaching animal rights enthusiasts, shrinking budgets at both the state and federal level, [and] netting."

By contrast, sportfishermen worry relatively little about "encroaching animal rights enthusiasts," and, as taxpayers, we regard "shrinking budgets at both the state and federal level" as a positive trend. Furthermore, Atlantic coastal fishermen are not inclined to link "dying habitats" and "deteriorating fisheries," since we know the principal reason our fisheries are deteriorating is incompetent management. And while state administrators urge still more people to buy still more fishing licenses to support still more biologists in the manner to which they've become accustomed, most anglers feel there're already too many of us in competition for what's left.

Biologists and sportsmen are on divergent paths in other respects as well. Anglers increasingly realize that size limits represent caps on an abundance of larger fish. Establish a striper size limit of eighteen inches, and most fish will soon be smaller than that. Raise the limit to twenty-eight inches, and eventually anglers will catch few fish larger than twenty-seven inches. And so on. That's why many people dislike all size restrictions. They prefer bag limits, in which each angler can decide what fish—if any—he wants to keep, regardless of size.

Biologists are like engineers in imagining they can fine-tune the workings of nature. Such fine-tuning, however, only works in computer models. In addition, almost every administrator—be he biologist or engineer—is unduly concerned with his authority and control over those beneath him, which in the case of any public agency includes the public. Although increasing numbers of anglers know better, state agencies are always trying to convince us that there'd be no fish without them. Very often, of course, the opposite is true: There'd be more fish without the heavy hand of government making sure that every last specimen is caught and accounted for. The most dangerous aspect of the myth that the state provides us with our fish is that most state and federal biologists believe it themselves. They truly imagine there'd be no striped bass without them—except when there *are* no striped bass, of course, and then pollution, weather, or other "natural causes" are to blame.

In the heat of midsummer in 1994, state biologists electroshocked a sampling of Roanoke stripers, put them into rectangular holding tanks—the shape of the tanks is important, because fish tend to congregate in the corners of rectangular tanks, where they may die of asphyxiation, while circular tanks encourage the fish to keep swimming and breathing normally—held the stripers for hours in the hot sun, and finally transported them to a totally different and warmer environment upstream. That any of these fish survived is testament to the hardiness of striped bass and their suitability for catch-and-release fishing. However, the state initially used the data it derived from this "experiment" to suggest that since so many striped bass had died, there was no way the North Carolina Wildlife Resource Commission could condone a Roanoke River catch-and-release fishery.

When the way the state had collected its data came to light, the commission was forced to redo the test. This time, the stripers were caught by anglers and held for three days in circular tanks in the nearby Weldon fish hatchery, into which fresh river water was continually pumped and drained away. In this test, the average mortality was only 6.5 percent. Interestingly, there was no appreciable difference between the mortality of stripers caught on live bait and those caught on artificial lures, even though a greater percentage of the fish caught on live bait were hooked deeper than those caught on the artificials. Deeper hooking, however, means more handling, a more frequent use of the hook disgorger, more lost slime, greater stress, and more potential fungal infections—particularly as water temperatures rise during the summer. Some of the deep-hooked and much-handled fish may have seemed all right when they were released after three days, but common sense suggests they suffered later. That's why a somewhat chastened North Carolina Wildlife Resources Commission recommended that catch-and-release anglers fish with single, barbless hooks and artificial lures rather than bait, and cease catch-and-release fishing once water temperatures rise to seventy-three degrees Fahrenheit when mortality levels begin to escalate.

Such refined concerns are moot, however, when a primary habitat is devastated. Five months after Lefty, Tom, and I departed the Roanoke amid much optimism concerning that year's spawning, a technocrat of the U.S. Army Corps of Engineers—his excuse and motto: "I didn't break any laws"—wiped out a significant portion of the upper river's 1989–95 year-classes of striped bass, plus uncounted catfish, perch, and shad.

After heavy early summer rains, the lakes behind the dams began to rise. Instead of relieving the pressure gradually—as the corps always claimed it could—the functionary flung open the gates on the night of July 28 and lowered Lake Gaston over four feet in less than twelve hours.

Chuck Laughridge wrote me just after the disaster: "There are so many words that whirl through my head when I contemplate this mess. *Stupid* and *negligent* are the most benign."

By the time state biologists finished counting dead stripers, they'd found more than twenty-four hundred belly-up just below the dam and another six to eight thousand swept into the bottomlands bordering the river, then stranded when the falling Roanoke retreated to its usual channels. The average weight of these fish was 3.9 pounds. Tens of thousands of smaller striped bass were scavenged by birds, raccoons, or 'possums, or ignored by commission workers who had their hands full dealing with the larger fish and the clouds of mosquitoes hatched by the flood.

Despite an intense but all too brief furor in the North Carolina press, no corps official was charged with incompetence or brought to account. It didn't help that the Atlantic States Marine Fisheries Commission's Striped Bass Stock Assessment Subcommittee looked at the Roanoke kill and decided it would have "no adverse impact" on the striper's overall recovery. The subcommittee even recommended maintaining all former quotas in the watershed. In time, everyone responsible has received, or will receive, his or her automatic pay raises, promotions, and retirement benefits. Yet the Roanoke Valley Striped Bass Coalition did manage to extract a consolation from the catastrophe. It persuaded a mildly guilt-ridden North Carolina

Wildlife Resources Commission to make the upper Roanoke a catch-and-release, barbless-hook-only fishery after April 1 each year, regardless of whether the upper river's kill quota has been achieved.

To see for myself what effect the fish kill had, I returned to the Roanoke in early May 1996. Fishing with Manteo guide Brian DeHart—a newcomer to the river who's hoping to supplement his Outer Banks income with early-spring fly fishing trips to the Roanoke—I caught a striper with my first cast and four more with my next five casts. The fish were small, however, and the largest striper I saw that afternoon and the next morning was a 4½-pounder caught on a fly by airline pilot Bill Wilkerson. Clearly, the previous summer's striper kill had affected the fishery. Quality fish capable of drawing anglers from all over the country were in short supply, if not nonexistent. Yet, since biologists are concerned only with quantity, not quality, and since the total poundage of stripers in the river (aka the biomass) is about the same as it was the previous year, the state thinks everything's fine.

The good news was the many new fly fishermen I saw. Whereas Lefty, Tom, and I had been the only fly fishermen on the river the previous spring, I counted eleven boats with fly fishermen in 1996. The most passionate of the lot was Chuck Laughridge himself, who'd apparently studied Lefty's techniques and was now laying out line half the width of the river. He said the Roanoke Valley Striped Bass Coalition wouldn't rest until the entire system is catch and release and the commercial quota is closed.

"Our proposal is not so much about *mortality*," said Chuck, "as it is about *morality* and the sportsman's desire to raise the ethical bar for all of us—even," he smiled, "people who work for the government."

# · 10 ·

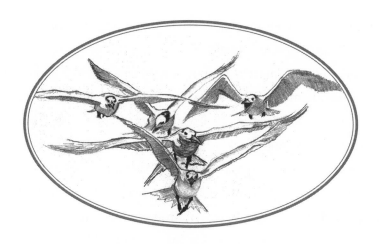

# THE CHESAPEAKE

I N 1864, A prominent Philadelphian named Thaddeus Norris
published *The American Angler's Book: Embracing the Natural
History of Sporting Fish, and the Art of Taking Them.* Perhaps because the book appeared at the height of the Civil War, Norris
decided to play down his southern roots. He was, after all, a
native Virginian, born in 1811 in Warrenton, seat of Fauquier
County. Accents may be lost, but the common names we learn
as children stay with us all our lives. So it was that Thaddeus
Norris preferred "rockfish" to "striped bass" in the book's only
anecdote pertinent to his youth in Virginia and written even as
Grant's army was laying siege to Petersburg: "Most tidewater
anglers have pleasant reminiscences of this fish, but no recol-
lection of bass fishing comes back to me with greater pleasure,
than my first essay among the 'big ones.' It was many years ago,
in the month of June, when on a visit to a relative—an ardent

though not a scientific angler—who lived on the banks of the broad Rappahannock, near its mouth. On the morning after my arrival, my host improvised a bout with the rockfish; and I saw from my chamber window, a negro boy, with no other implement than a four-pronged stick, capture as many soft crabs as sufficed for bait and breakfast. Our canoes were staked out some distance from the margin of the sandy beach, which made it necessary to be carried to them. This task was speedily accomplished by a sturdy little negro; who with trousers rolled up on his sable drumsticks, dumped the whole cargo—bait, rods and four anglers—into two 'dug outs.' We were soon staked down on the flats, a half mile from the shore, where the water was six feet deep. Our object was, to place the boats in such a position, as to fish into the 'galls,' or bare places, where there was no grass; these were of various sizes, from three rods square to half an acre.

"The rods, reels and scientific tackle of the city anglers, excited the wonder, and no doubt the silent contempt of the native fishermen; who were rigged, one with a hand-line, and the other with a stout cedar pole, with a line attached to it, that might have held a shark. My host, a staunch Democrat and anti-bank man, dubbed my rod, which was not over stout and fifteen feet long, 'The Nick Biddle[1] pole,' and assured me it was

---

[1]Nicholas Biddle (1786–1844) was a Philadelphia financier appointed by President Monroe to be a director of the Bank of the United States in 1819, and elected its president in 1822. When Andrew Jackson entered the White House in 1828, he initiated a campaign against the bank that ended in his second term with his veto of the bank's charter and withdrawal of all federal funds. Biddle got a state charter and reopened the bank on March 1, 1836, as "The Bank of the United States of Pennsylvania," but in 1839, he resigned and retired. This dispute helps date Norris's story to the mid-1830s.

all well enough for white perch, but would not hold a rockfish, such as he could bring with a strong pull, and a 'whop,' right into the canoe.

"It was my good fortune to hook the first fish, a fine fellow of six pounds. There was much laughter, of course; Uncle Rolly declared I would never get him in. 'See how your pole bends! Why he's way off in the middle of the gall already! Why don't you pull him in?' The old man was here interrupted by the disappearance of his pine-bark float, and in less time than it takes to tell it, he had his fish flapping in the bottom of the canoe. 'There!' said he, 'I can catch ten to your one. I tell you, your Nick Biddle pole will never do here!' By this time I had my fish pretty well in hand, and after a dash or two more, Jordan, the negro boy, put a wide crab-net under him, and lifted him in. The next fish Uncle Rolly hooked broke his hold; so did a good many more, and large ones too; while every fish struck by the dandy pole, was killed artistically, though the old man thought with much unnecessary ceremony. At the ebb of the tide, science had told. We had a good time of it, and the owner of the 'Biddle pole' felt great confidence in his fine tackle, and much quiet satisfaction in his first success with it; while Uncle Rolly laughed at his tactics. We went home and ate the stewed head and shoulders of a large rockfish and soft crabs for dinner. Next day we tried our luck again with equal success; and before leaving for home one of the town anglers killed a rockfish of twenty-five pounds, which Uncle Rolly would certainly have lost."

When local anglers mention striper fishing in the Chesapeake watershed, they may be thinking of different things. They could mean bait fishing in the "galls," as Norris did, or fly fishing in skinny water using push-poled boats and other techniques originally developed for flats fishing in Florida. Or they could be thinking of sitting up all night in the chilly spring, watching a lantern-illuminated rod tip and occasionally getting a nod from a young striper that's just moved into the shallows from a deep wintering hole. Or they could mean chumming in a fleet of anchored boats, like some inland-sea version of the bluefishing armadas that once dominated the New York Bight. Chesapeake anglers may be as competitive as the trollers who curse and dodge one another close by the pilings of the Bay Bridge-Tunnel, or as contemplative as Ellington White in his essay "Striped Bass and Southern Solitude."

Unlike the cases of trout and salmon, with their many stories and books, little that qualifies as literature is written about striped bass. There's much hard-core information about the fish, and such books and articles serve the purpose of introducing novices to the sport. But what I mean by "literature" is writing that resonates with the aesthetics of nature and angling. Contrast, for example, most of the where-to and how-to stuff you've read about stripers with these observations by Ellington White from the October 10, 1966, issue of *Sports Illustrated:* "The best way to fish is alone. The best time to fish is the fall. Believing these simple truths to be selfevident, I set out alone each fall to fish the rivers and creeks that flow out of Virginia into the Chesapeake Bay. It is a good time of year all around. Everybody else in the world is watching a football game. Leaves cover the roadside beer cans, and the traffic is light. . . .

"I don't know of any fish that gives as much pleasure to as many fishermen as the ubiquitous striper. He may not be as dazzling as a bonefish or as much a roughneck as a snook, but he covers more ground than these fish do and so comes into contact with more people. There is nothing provincial about him, either. He can get along in fresh water just as well as he can in salt water, river water as well as ocean water, shallow water or deep water—it's all the same to him. People fish for him in boats, on banks, in the surf or by wading. They use trolling rods, boat rods, casting rods, spinning rods, fly rods and every kind of bait made—wood, plastic, feathered and live. And he survives them all. Praise the striper . . . the most democratic fish that swims. . . .

"Stripers seem to regard the bay as a school they have to complete before graduating into the Atlantic Ocean. The school lasts four years. A few dropouts may tackle the ocean sooner than that, but the majority are content to wait until graduation day. Then they are ready to join the big ocean community on the outside. . . . The young striper just out of school tends to stay pretty close to home for the first year or so, but as his size increases so does his boldness, and off he goes to prowl the New England coast, 700 miles away. In the fall he frequently returns, packing weights of twenty and thirty pounds. It is a curious fact that stripers reach the bay about the same time that alumni are arriving in Charlottesville, Virginia, to watch Mr. Jefferson's eleven take another licking, but if you think that homecoming is worth watching you ought to see what happens when the Old Boys get together in the bay. It's an alumni secretary's dream. Gulls throw up tents all over the place, covering the big feeds, and the campus becomes one huge thrashing contest. Before long the racket reaches shore, and here comes a fleet of fishermen pounding out to join in the fun.

"It's great sport if you like that sort of thing, and most striper fishermen do, but not caring for homecomings myself, in Charlottesville or the bay, I cut the motor and drift into the shallows behind Rigby Island. It's quieter there. You can hear the tide running through the grass. I toss out the anchor, rig up a rod, stuff my pockets with flies, climb into a pair of boots and wade off in search of a few first-graders."

Ellington White fished the Chesapeake each fall partly to celebrate the bay's fecundity, partly to do penance for the sins we all accumulate over the previous months. I fish the bay for those reasons, but I also fish there because the Chesapeake is my Big Two-Hearted River.

The connection began in the summer of 1965 while I was learning Vietnamese in Washington, D.C. I made an overnight canoe trip down the Patuxent with another naval ensign. At dawn, I fished a small orange and black-spotted swimming plug by our campsite and caught a striper, and we ate it for breakfast. Every serendipitous detail of that trip contributed to its idyll, but the catching and consumption of that striped bass was a kind of communion. Like the Patuxent, I became bonded to the bay.

After my first tour in Vietnam, I was sent to the Naval Academy, where I gradually took over the courses of an English professor dying of cancer. By March 1967, he was gone, and I was running four sections of plebe English, one upper-class course, and a volunteer class in basic Vietnamese (Oliver North was one of my students). Pursuing striped bass was so convenient that I was sometimes able to catch fish in the ten-minute intervals between classes.

At that time, the Naval Academy laundry was located adjacent to the Severn River, into which it daily pumped tons of warm water and starch. Carp crowded into the outfall pipe to ingest the starch, while, in the early spring, small stripers hung near the surface in the flume of warm water. I could never get the little guys to do more than swirl at a popper, but they'd often roll up into a streamer just as I began to lift and speed up the line for another cast. It was exactly as Thaddeus Norris had observed a century earlier: The striper "follows and seizes the fly *under* rather than *on* the surface, and does not start from the bottom with a spring as the Trout or Salmon."

Stripers also lay in the shadow line below the academy's playing field lights at night. Sometimes in the early-morning hours when I was afraid to sleep for fear of dreaming, I'd go to the seawall by myself, kneel to keep my shadow below the parallel of perfect darkness, and cast to where submerged rubble caused a slight eddy in the current. I fished white streamers, instead of black, because I didn't know any better, and once in a while I caught a striped bass, because it didn't know any better either.

By June 1967, I was back in I Corps as a team leader, conducting taped and later transcribed interrogations of North Vietnamese prisoners for a RAND Corporation "motivation and moral study" of the enemy. Our final question was always, "What would you do if we let you go?" The prisoners' answers were always the same: "I'd kill you; we won't stop killing Americans until the last of you hairy, long-nosed apes have left Vietnam." Then I learned that White House advisor Walt Rostow was cutting off the concluding question and answer and giving the edited interviews to Lyndon Johnson. Since most prisoners had previously admitted to considerable fear and suffering along the Ho Chi Minh Trail, the final Q and A were essential to understanding the depth of North Vietnam's determination to prevail. But Walt Rostow wanted the president to believe in the same illusionary light at the end of the tunnel that Rostow himself thought he saw.

When I got back to Annapolis that fall—"Have a good summer vacation?" a colleague innocently asked—I was so busy with teaching and fishing that the war soon became only a background of occasionally seen headlines—except at night, when I still dreamed in Vietnamese. After class, I often launched my aluminum cartop boat from the seaplane ramp across the Severn River, then—depending on the time, tide, and wind—either worked poppers across the "galls" of the grass beds around Greenbury Point or ran to the Bay Bridge, where I found stripers feeding on the surface or holding close to pilings, where they'd attack almost any bucktail I free-spooled down to them.

Another option was to sail a Naval Academy sloop to the drop-off near Thomas Point Lighthouse, anchor, and start a chum line of inexpensive manoe (soft-shelled) clams. Sailing to a fishing ground may seem romantic, but a centerboard sloop is a lousy angling platform. If I pulled up the centerboard, the boat swung too widely on its anchor for my companions and me to maintain a proper chum line; if I left the centerboard down, hooked fish would sometimes snag our lines on it, no matter how far over the side we jabbed our rods to clear them.

But there was a larger worry. As the sun sets in the late summer on the Chesapeake, the wind usually dies with it. The brisk breeze that carried us so swiftly to Thomas Point became a gnat-laden stillness by dusk. We had to either quit fishing just when it was getting best to ride the last zephyrs back to the dock, or hope we could get a tow from a powerboat heading to the harbor. One evening, a fellow instructor in the English, History and Government Department—what the midshipmen called "Bull"—and I had to pull up the floorboards and use them as paddles, a course of action that didn't get us back until after midnight with a mess of stripers we were too tired to clean. I still chummed after that, but I always made sure the boat I boarded had an engine.

After I was posted to the Paris Peace Talks in December 1968, I realized how much I missed the Chesapeake. No amount of work in Annapolis had ever overloaded my circuitry the way fourteen-hour days at our Paris embassy did. At least in Maryland, I'd always been able to sneak off for a few casts from the seawall. My newfound friends in the Trout, Grayling and Salmon Society of France took me fly fishing in Normandy, and Charles Ritz once had me to lunch at his hotel, where he dismayed other guests by jumping up to demonstrate the action of his latest parabolic rod design. But such kindnesses were formal, and I missed the spontaneity of my Annapolis outings.

By June 1969, I was exhausted by work that wasn't making any sense or difference. I decided to quit the navy and marry the girl I liked best before somebody else did, and for the two of us to find a farm near the Chesapeake. Yet I wasn't prepared for the culture shock of coming home. One morning I carried two clearances above Top Secret and was privy to information not even the president knew; the next evening I was sitting alone with a jet-lag high in the Naval Academy BOQ wardroom, watching *The Tonight Show* while Johnny Carson and his celebrity guests, Buddy Hackett and Sammy Davis Jr., cracked wise about our delegation's doings. It was dismaying for me to realize that the Vietnam War had become just another entertainment, and that the sarcasm of Carson and company would likely have more influence on the pace of the Peace Talks than anything I'd done or could do.

By October 1972, Barbara and I had our farm, if not *on* the Chesapeake—we couldn't afford that—then within a few miles. My first book—*Zane Grey: Outdoorsman*—had sold well; my second—*Profiles in Saltwater Angling*—was about to come out. I'd also moved from the boating and outdoor editorship of *Popular Mechanics* in New York City to a senior editorship at *National Wildlife* and *International Wildlife* in Washington, D.C. Meanwhile, my erstwhile colleagues at the Peace Talks had finally begun to make some headway toward exchanging prisoners and signing an accord just in time for the presidential election—exactly as I'd predicted would happen before leaving Paris three years earlier.

The week before the election I joined fellow outdoor writer Boyd Pfeiffer and his friends Irv Swope and Joe Zimmer at Tilghman Island, Maryland, for what turned out to be my last, best striped bass fishing for the next eighteen years. We stayed at Harrison's Chesapeake House, which has been owned and operated by the same family since 1875, and used two boats to range the bay between Poplar Island and the mouth of the Choptank. Boyd and I shared his boat; he's right-handed, and I'm left-. Whenever we spotted diving birds and raced in their direction, Boyd would stand to starboard and stream half his fly line over his right shoulder, while I'd stand to port and stream half my line over my left. We'd run downwind, swing into place, kill the engine, and shoot the works.

In those days, the Chesapeake always had ample stocks of baby 'bunker and bay anchovies. So long as we kept our boats on the fringe of the action, stripers and bluefish would stay up for long minutes, chasing down all the prey they found. In ideal situations—and there were many such that October—the four of us were alone on the bay, but surrounded by acres of breaking fish. After the schools worked beyond easy casting range, we'd reel in, start up, swing wide to where we thought the fish were moving, and cut the engines again.

The sight and sound of so many swirling-splashing fish was exhilarating, even without hookups. Panic-stricken baitfish dashed to the apparent safety of our drifting hulls, and we had easy casting to the pursuing predators. The trick was to cast to swirls—more likely to be made by stripers than bluefish, with their characteristic slashing smashes—and then not twitch the streamer. Since bluefish feed more aggressively and generally higher in the water column than striped bass, a sinking fly was less likely to attract their attention. There's nothing wrong with a bluefish on a fly. Indeed, they often jump and usually show more razzle-dazzle than a striper of equivalent size. The problem is they'll chew up a fly even when they don't bite it off. Furthermore, we each planned to keep a few fish, and white-fleshed stripers were generally preferred at home to the darker, oily bluefish.

By 1972, bluefish were already more abundant in the Chesapeake than striped bass. For every striper we caught that October, we hooked two or three blues. It's ironic—and possibly significant—that bluefish flourished in the Chesapeake throughout the '70s and well into the '80s, but began to disappear at about the time stripers started their comeback. Perhaps the decline of the voracious, slammer-sized blues helped facilitate the recovery of younger stripers. Today, autumn schools of gamefish in the mid-Chesapeake are almost all striped bass.

But they don't stay on the surface as reliably or as long as they did in 1972—possibly because baitfish are generally scarcer, and boats chasing the stripers are more numerous. The most dramatic action off Tilghman Island now comes in the spring during the so-called trophy season.

In early May 1995, I went fishing aboard Buddy Harrison's *Pleasure Merchant.* Each of the eight anglers he carried that day was legally allowed to keep one fish at least thirty-two inches long. When spring trophy fishing recommenced in 1991—the year after Maryland's five-year striped bass fishing moratorium ended—the minimum size for a keeper was thirty-six inches. Anglers complained that there weren't enough of these eleven-year-old fish to satisfy their desire to take home one apiece. They thought that by pressuring the state to lower the standard, they'd catch more. Instead, they caught the same number, but were able to keep all the thirty-two- to thirty-six-inch fish they'd formerly had to release. In the process, they radically reduced the number of capital breeders for future production and bumper year-classes.

Even Buddy Harrison is no longer sure the trophy season is such a good idea. The success of his century-old inn depends on return business—meaning satisfied customers. When the state's Department of Natural Resources (DNR) decided to reopen the spring trophy season, it based its decision on the antiquated assumption that big stripers are expendable. Yet they're clearly not expendable to either optimum spawning or quality angling. From 1991 to 1995, the catch per angler effort of trophy-sized fish dropped dramatically. Harrison's charter fleet has excellent guides, but most customers still went home fishless. Our party of eight was fortunate to catch three keepers. Those of us who didn't get to crank one in said we'd had a great time, but good sports always say that.

State biologists continually project the availability of more striped bass than fishermen can find. That's why, in 1995, Maryland's DNR decided to lower the minimum "trophy striper" size to twenty-six inches, and extend the spring fishery into the Fourth of July weekend. Many more fish were killed, of course, and many more anglers said they were satisfied. But that satisfaction was obtained at the cost of quality fishing in the future.

Resource administrators acknowledge that during the 1960s, recreational fishing for striped bass was worth half a billion dollars annually to coastal communities from Maine to the Chesapeake. That figure is potentially five times greater today. Yet administrators refuse to make any connection between the frenzied fishing of the late '60s and '70s and the subsequent collapse of striper stocks—or even to consider the possibility that such a collapse could happen again. According to current estimates, there are 538,000 resident anglers fishing the Maryland portion of the Chesapeake, plus 580,690 residents fishing the Virginia portion. That's more than 1.1 million recreational fishermen in pursuit of the same limited number of bay stripers. Exactly how many fish are there? Despite the posturing of biologists in both states, no one has the least idea. Whatever the number, it's impossible that there're enough stripers to satisfy 1.1 million anglers so long as each expects to take home several daily limits a year.

Half a century ago, Maryland pioneered the concept of a minimum/maximum "slot limit" for striped bass. That concept still holds the key to sustainable quality fishing. Unfortunately, Maryland's current management is based on the notion that it's better to have lots of smaller fish in the system than an optimum distribution of all age groups. Starting in 1985, when it shut down all forms of striped bass fishing for five years, Maryland led other Atlantic states in adopting significant conservation measures to rebuild coastal populations. Now it's leading the charge to replunder the resource. This is sadly ironic when we realize that the rockfish has been so much a part of Maryland history, the state seal is divided between a tobacco farmer and a waterman holding a striped bass.

# · 11 ·

# SOUTHERN NEW ENGLAND

Although Nelson Bryant was born in Red Bank, New Jersey, in 1923, he caught his first fish on Martha's Vineyard, and that's made all the difference: He's never wanted to live anywhere else. Shortly before the Battle of the Bulge, where Nelson was wounded for the second time since parachuting into France the night before D-Day, he received a V-mail boost from his dad, who'd just caught a mess of schoolie stripers on trout flies in the Vineyard's Tisbury Great Pond.

After the war, Nelson got work as a deckhand on the research schooner *Reliance,* based in Woods Hole. In old New Englandish, a *hole* is neither a hole nor a harbor, but a channel between two islands. In a sense, then, the oceanic arm between Woods Hole and Martha's Vineyard became Nelson's Big Two-Hearted River. He kept a cheap Herter fly rod and Pflueger reel aboard the *Reliance,* which is why the tackle was near at hand when a school of Atlantic bonito suddenly surfaced one day in Woods Hole harbor. Nelson cast the already attached fly—a Mickey Finn—hooked a seven-pound bonito, and somehow, despite the thicket of pilings around the schooner, landed the fish. When Joe Brooks caught his fly-rod-record striper, Nelson resolved to top it.

"First, I decided to get as much information as I could," he recalls. "I wrote Harold Gibbs, who was Rhode Island's fish and game administrator and who, with his brother, Frank, were the best-known saltwater fly rodders in New England. I asked Gibbs for any tips. He had just two: 'Use three feet of anything for a leader and make sure your streamer is a blue-and-white bucktail.'"

Nelson fished by bike for two weeks along the summer-sheltered north shore of Martha's Vineyard without a strike. Then one balmy night, he fell asleep on the beach and awoke around three in the morning, dew-soaked and chilled. He decided to warm up by making a few casts in the pitch darkness before heading home. On his very first try, he hooked and landed a six-pound striper. On his next cast, he hooked and landed an eight-pounder. Then a twelve-pounder. Then a fourteen-pounder. Then he got such a jolting strike, followed by such a heavy run, that he thought a shark must have moved in among the stripers and taken his fly by mistake. The fish pulled out nearly all of Nelson's backing before turning parallel to the beach to swim back and forth, with Nelson recovering a few feet of line and steering the fish a little

closer to shore with each reversal. When the fish lay just beyond the lapping surf, the reel fell off the rod. Fortunately,
the fish was so beat that it waited for Nelson to fumble
around by his feet, find the reel, and reattach it to the butt.
Then Nelson waded in with his flashlight to see what he'd
hooked.

He couldn't believe his eyes. There lay a striped bass of at
least thirty pounds! A new world record! As Nelson reached
out to grab the fish by the jaw, the fly popped out. The great
striper rolled upright and swam slowly out of sight. Nelson decided it was time to go back to Dartmouth and get a degree—
a step that eventually led to his thirty-year career as an outdoor
columnist for the *New York Times*.

I thought of the many unanticipated paths a writer takes as
I trudged behind Nelson over the dunes from what he calls his
"parking lot"—actually an undeveloped homesite that he and
a dozen other anglers have purchased to have someplace to
leave their cars while fishing Dogfish Bar, near the western end
of Lobsterville Beach. Behind us trailed Arthur Hendrick, an
old friend who has fished with me from Yellowstone Park to
Honduras, and Eric Peterson, who was born decades after the
rest of us but is already something of a fly-fishing guru, with
his own fly shop in Fairfield, Connecticut, and a waiting list
of clients eager to have him take them bonefishing in the
Bahamas.

One difference between sportsmen born before World War
II—like Arthur, Nelson, and me—and those born since is that,

whereas many of us in the prewar generation dreamed of selling a story or two to a major outdoor magazine and even—dare we hope for so much?—one day having a regular column, the anglers of Eric's generation more often dream of having their own TV shows.

Although Arthur Hendrick travels enough, and is knowledgeable and handsome enough, to have a TV show, he instead makes an occasional contribution to the New York Anglers' Club bulletin. His greatest angling adventures seem to come when he cartops his twelve-foot, Bart Hauthaway canoe to fly fish offshore areas that not even the strongest double-hauler on the beach can reach, and near-shore shallows where not even the most intrepid motorboater would follow.

Arthur characterized our autumn 1995 trip to the Vineyard as the best fishing he's done without catching a fish. Eric described the Vineyard visit as a "treat," but primarily for the chance to hear us old-timers swap tales. Eric is young enough to be still building memories, while Arthur, Nelson, and I increasingly derive pleasure in the present by recalling fond moments from the past.

Although none of us hooked a fish during our trip to Dogfish Bar, Nelson recalled an epiphany from an evening outing the previous June. Just as he'd crossed the last dune, he'd seen what he believed to be the light of countless fireflies flickering for more than a mile down the beach. Almost instantly, however, he'd realized it wasn't insects at all, but the backcast-striking of dozens of hooks on the rocks behind a shoulder-to-shoulder line of fly fishermen.

Between catching a fish under those conditions and having a fishless beach to ourselves, we older anglers preferred the solitude of the seascape bounded by the distant lights of Menemsha, Gay Head, and a very few residences on the Elizabeth Islands across Vineyard Sound. We shared the sensation that comes to all people on a deserted beach that we were the only humans on earth. I stood thigh-deep in the gentle surf and cast to a slough while twilight stole color from the sea. When darkness shrank the radius of my existence to just the length of the fly rod in my hands, I reeled in and joined the others for the trek back to Nelson's parking lot.

The first saltwater fishing clubs anywhere on earth were born on the shores of Rhode Island and Massachusetts in the 1830s. Yet it took more than another century for New England anglers to connect fly fishing with the sea and turn the combination into the phenomenon—or should I say religion?—that saltwater fly fishing has become throughout the region today. Ironically, the coast of southern New England is peppered with spots for striper fly fishing just as good as the Potomac falls where this sport began. The Rhode Island author of *Striper Moon*, J. Kenney Abrames, does most of his fly fishing from shore. "I'm not sure why," he wrote. "I think it has to do with intimacy. There is a quiet measured pace to fishing when you stand in one place and watch the water rise and fall. You begin to notice things you could not see if you were passing by. Walking takes time, but it does not waste it." Most fly fishermen would agree, but only those in New England have the luxury of many deep-water points and beaches where anglers in bobbing boats are at a disadvantage.

One of the reasons it took New Englanders more than a century to link fly fishing and striped bass was the old attitude that fly tackle is for trout and salmon only. Some nineteenth-century sportsmen were scandalized—not only that Daniel Webster had degraded salmon flies by using them to catch mere "food fishes" such as striped bass, mackerel, and cod, but also that he'd boasted of it. They regarded salmon as the ultimate "upstairs" species, while the striper was clearly "downstairs." Why, they rhetorically asked, would anyone fish flies for pedestrian stripers when he could and should be pursuing the king of fishes?

Fresh-run salmon do make glorious leaps—but not because they're morally superior to striped bass, only because they're genetically coded to do so in order to traverse the many rapids and small falls on their spawning runs. Once a salmon ejects its eggs or milt, its inclination to leap shuts down, and overwintering Atlantic salmon do little more than wrestle and roll when hooked.

Stripers jump infrequently—and hardly ever when hooked—because they don't need to; they spawn below the fall line. In their ability to use current, however—to sheer downstream (or downtide) and take line—striped bass are as capable as salmon. Fighting ability is, thus, a function of a fish's biology, not its spirituality. Just as a tuna in shallow water or a bonefish in deep water is equally out of its depth from the angler's point of view—since both can be subdued in a fraction of the time it

takes to catch a deep-water tuna or a shallow-water bonefish—
a salmon or a striped bass caught in the referenceless realm of
the open ocean resists in a confused and hapless manner that
contrasts markedly with a salmon hooked in a swift river or a
striper hooked in the surf.

In the same vein, too many anglers compare the difficulty
they have in persuading an Atlantic salmon to take a fly with
the relative ease with which a striped bass can be hooked on
just about anything. They call the striper "dumb." Yet comparing a fasting salmon—whose spawning-run programming
doesn't include food—with a striper in a feeding frenzy, or
even one stationed by a jetty, where every smaller creature
swimming by is at risk, is not just confusing apples with or-
anges, it's comparing pomegranates with tomatoes.

It's equally erroneous to suggest that, because striped bass
have a potential life span measured in decades, while salmon
don't live more than four or five years, a twenty-year-old
striper must be smarter than the biggest salmon. The longevity
of a fish is a matter of luck, not intelligence. The fifty-pound
striper that has been caught and released a dozen times is no
wiser when it comes to inhaling the thirteenth lure than an Atlantic salmon would be had it the same capacity for recreational recycling.

Still, the most important reason it took so long for saltwater fly fishing to catch on was the lack of proper tackle. For
starters, stripers in New England are generally larger than
those caught south of Delaware Bay. In 1892, Francis Endicott
characterized any striper weighing "six pounds or less" caught

from one of the iron stands at Newport, Rhode Island, as a "minnow." Yet even such "minnows" would have been challenge enough for a nineteenth-century fly fisherman with a bamboo wand and horsehair leader.

That began to change in 1832, when Captain Lester Crandall of Ashaway, Rhode Island, began providing tarred-cotton handlines to members of an informal striped bass club on Massachusetts's Cuttyhunk Island. The members switched to rods and reels in the early 1840s, and Captain Crandall began importing Irish linen to make a stronger and finer-diameter twisted line for superior storage and casting. Meanwhile, in Kentucky, a group of watchmakers—beginning in 1810 with George Snyder, and peaking in the decades before the Civil War with Benjamin C. Milan and brothers Jonathan and Benjamin Meek—developed multiplying reels, whose jewel-geared spools revolved three or, in later models, four times with each turn of the handle. These reels were so precisely crafted and durable that they've only recently been surpassed by reels with magnetized ball bearings, which provide better drag control and predictable casts.

Prior to the multiplier, bait fishermen were forced to "strip-cast"—meaning that, much like fly fishermen, they'd strip coils from a reel and let them spiral down at their feet, or hold the loops in one hand, then lob the bait or lure with a sideways motion of the rod. In fly fishing, the weight of the line casts a relatively weightless fly; in strip-casting, the weight of the bait does the job. With single-action reels, the most anyone could toss a bait or lure was about sixty feet—and that only if he were tossing downwind. The genius of the Kentucky watchmakers was that they created a spool that not only stored line, but also turned so smoothly and easily that lures could be cast directly from the reel. Then the line could be retrieved at a rate almost equaling that of a handliner. A mere flick of the finger was enough to spin the handle of a Snyder reel a dozen or more revolutions. Yet a Snyder reel was so sturdy that one George made for the Honorable Brutus Clay in 1821 was still being used by the judge's descendants in the 1940s, when it was finally retired as a family heirloom.

Kentucky reels, however, were not really suitable for salt water. The Cuttyhunk Islanders needed reels made as precisely as a Snyder, but strengthened with corrosion-resistant brass and German silver (a nickel alloy). They were not to get such reels until the 1850s, when the brothers Julius and Edward vom Hofe started the first assembly-line reel factory in Brooklyn, New York. All early vom Hofe reels were made specifically for striped bass fishing. Consequently, as one of the company's ads put it, the reels were of the "finest quality rubber and German silver, full steel pivot with German silver bands, S-shaped balance handle to screw off, sliding oil cap, [and] tension click spring." Pressure was applied to the line with a "thumb stall" worn by the angler, or by a leather "check" attached to one of the reinforcing pillars. Early vom Hofe reels had no internal braking system, and, without a free-spool lever, anglers could get their knuckles severely rapped by the reel handle when a strong fish took off. With this and many other such problems to work out, it took much of the nineteenth century to develop conventional tackle suitable for saltwater use. No wonder it took much of the twentieth century to do the same for fly-fishing gear.

In the decade before the Civil War, striped bass fishing piers were built at various points along Long Island Sound, with the most prestigious at Newport, Point Judith, Squibnocket, Block Island, West Island, Pasque Island, and Montauk Point. Many of these piers were owned by individuals; some by members of a club. All locations were valuable, and several were sold and resold for sums equivalent to millions of modern dollars. Winans' Stand on Brenton Reef near Newport was one such pier. Another was the rock pile at Narragansett known as "Anthonys" in honor of the local innkeeper, John Anthony, who caught the first stripers there.

Angling success in the nineteenth century was measured less by the capture of individually large fish than by seasonal totals. For example, Francis Endicott did not cite any particular fish caught by Thomas Winans and his nephew, Thomas Whistler, during the summer they fished together from their Newport pier. Endicott reported only that the two landed 124 bass weighing 2,921 pounds for an average weight of 23 pounds per fish.

Modern anglers hear that the old striped bass clubs occasionally used lobster for bait or chum and assume this valuable shellfish must have been superior to what we use today. However, nineteenth-century fisherman got their best results from the same baits and chum we commonly use—namely, live eels, crabs, and menhaden. Indeed, Robert Barnwell Roosevelt even complained that lobster bait is "deficient in tenacity, and has to be tied on." Availability—then as now—was the most important factor in determining what bait was used. Since eels were regarded as a delicacy by nineteenth-century gourmands, and lobsters were not, it was often easier to catch sufficient lobsters for bait than eels. In the last year of the Civil War, Roosevelt warned anglers sailing to New England that "there is often great difficulty in obtaining bait, particularly during a storm, which is the time that it is most needed, as the fish bite best in rough weather, and on going from the cities it is well to pack a few hundred menhaden in a box with ice and sawdust, and this insures a supply for some days ahead."

Members of the Pasque Island Club had the best solution to this perennial problem. Genio C. Scott described this fraternity as encompassing "more than a thousand acres, which the club has divided into two farms, erected commodious buildings, including club-house, ice-house, stabling, etc. The club has also vegetable and flower gardens, sail-boats, and row-boats, *and the [tidal] river, which sets back a mile into the island, is stocked with a hundred-thousand menhaden as bait for the use of the club* [emphasis added]."

Old club records may document the members' names and the sizes of the fish they caught, but our best accounts of what it was like to fish there come through the pens of visitors. In the case of bygone New England striper clubs, we're fortunate to have had Genio C. Scott, who devoted fourteen pages of his *Fishing in American Waters* to "Angling at the

Bassing Clubs." An English doctor-friend accompanied Scott on a tour, first to West Island—"the most attractive five-acre island in America"; then to Cuttyhunk—formally incorporated as a club in 1865; to Pugne, or Penikese—owned by the eccentric millionaire John Anderson, who cared little for angling, but later gave the island to Louis Agassiz (along with $50,000) to operate a summer school for promising young marine naturalists; and to Pasque Island—"the *ne plus ultra* of a place for angling."

Most clubs maintained the same daily schedule. In the evening, members would draw for their next morning's stand. Some piers were obviously better at certain tides or seasons than others, but neither a member's wealth nor his social position ever affected the luck of his draw. Guests, however, were automatically given the best stands. Scott noted that this was "a feature of all the bassing clubs [and] on the morrow we will try to do honor to their estimate of us."

Even before sunrise, the gaffers—equivalent to British ghillies—were out chumming their particular stands. Often, by the time the anglers finished their first cups of tea or coffee and arrived at their assigned piers, stripers were boiling in the slick. The gaffers baited hooks, cast the lines of novices, and used the long handles of their gaffs to steer anglers' lines away from the rocks when a hooked fish threatened to snag. Other than these chores—plus gaffing, carrying, and weighing the fish—a gaffer wasn't allowed to aid an angler while he was fighting a fish. Indeed, no one but the angler was ever permitted to touch the tackle once a fish was hooked.

Some gaffers, however, felt free to offer advice. Mr. Mosier—the gaffer drawn by Genio Scott and his doctor-friend at West Island—was especially free in this regard. After making droll comments about everything from the hooks the anglers had brought to the way Scott fought his first fish, Mosier gaffed the forty-pounder and started in on the doctor: "You jist make a cast out into the Rifle Pit, and do it right away, for I see by their whirls that they are hungry." When the doctor immediately hooked a fish, Mosier got more excited than the doctor: "He breaks water; I seen him; he's a scrough!" After the twenty-pounder was landed, Mosier rather impatiently told Scott and the doctor: "Gentlemen, the breakfast horns has been blowin a good while."

All anglers were expected to go in for breakfast, which, according to Scott, was "the morning's trysting-place for the members of the club, where they recount their exploits over their tea and coffee, with broiled bluefish, striped bass, and scopogue [porgy] or with broiled chicken and beefsteak, . . . and the stories of successful taken by some, and of parting tackle with others."

On Cuttyhunk Island, if an angler tired of pier fishing, he could always try the trout preserve (catch and release only) or fish two different ponds for black bass and white perch. Pasque Island—nine miles long, two miles wide, and separated from the nearest other land by half a mile of water—was "stocked with all the English and Scotch game birds and most of their game animals, including also several hundred American [white-tailed] deer, prairie-fowl [heath hen?], etc."

When Scott and the doctor wanted to vary their saltwater sport, they sailed off to harpoon swordfish, "still-baited for squeteague [weakfish] weighing five to fifteen pounds each," and "if the bluefish came in such shoals as to turn our strait into a state of commotion resembling soap suds, we rigged to the end of our bass line about two feet of piano wire, on which we wound a hook with copper wire. Then we anchored on the edge of the tide and cast out a hook baited without much care, and the moment afterward we were saluted by a jerk and a somersault a yard clear of the surface, and a short, vigorous fight to bring the bluefish to gaff. An hour of energetic sport, and twenty bluefish of from eight to twelve pounds each generally satisfied us."

Scott's doctor-friend was so impressed by his tour of the Elizabeth Islands that he left for England determined to return when he retired and live on Pasque. Scott described the archipelago as to "be numbered with the watering-places of the world *par excellence*. While aquatic birds skim the waves, and the gulls are screaming, dipping, and darting over a shoal of bluefish or menhaden, vessels outward and homeward bound are always passing, for it includes in its range of view the packets and steamers for England, and the steam and sailing crafts between New York and Boston. We have here the foreground and perspective worthy the pencil of Claude de Lorraine, while the background is formed of the granite shores of Massachusetts, with its improvements so varied and important as to give surety of an intelligent and industrious population. Who would not delight to angle here?"

In the 1890s, Atlantic stocks of striped bass collapsed under relentless fishing pressure all along the coast. Gill nets intercepted the fish on their spawning runs; seines surrounded them on their wintering grounds. Burgeoning cities teemed with laborers and immigrants willing to pay a few pennies per pound for even the stalest fish. Any striped bass not sold fresh to a downtown restaurant could be peddled by pushcart through the tenements a week later. By 1907, the last of the Elizabeth Island striper clubs—the Cuttyhunk Fishing Association—was disbanded for lack of fish.

The few fish that survived this piscatorial pogrom grew exceptionally large. In 1913, Charles B. Church drifted a live eel through Quick's Hole between Nashawena and Pasque Islands and caught a seventy-three-pound striped bass. That world-record fish fueled the imaginations of New England anglers for the next two generations.

In 1952, Winifred ("Win") Brooks wrote a best-selling novel, *The Shining Tides,* about an even larger striped bass. Although the book's human characters were clearly based on real Bostonians and Cape Codders whom Brooks knew through his work as sports editor of the now defunct *Herald-American*—his weekly angling column appeared under the byline "Dark Montreal"—Brooks used an author's note to deny it. He also used the note to talk about Roccus, his hundred-pound striped bass protagonist on her last journey north. Some readers, unaware of the North Carolina giant caught in a net in 1891 and weighing 125 pounds, doubted that striped bass could ever reach such a huge size. Others questioned the big striper's ability to jump. To the latter, Brooks enigmatically replied, "Though some may challenge her leaping in the strict sense of the word, she leaps because many years ago in the Weweantic I saw her leave her natural element."

The all-tackle sportfishing striped bass record is now a seventy-eight-pound, eight-ounce fish caught on September 21, 1982, at Atlantic City, New Jersey. Both this fish and Church's long-standing record were caught in decades when stripers were in decline. Older fish were able to survive longer and grow larger then, because fewer people were fishing for them. Church's striper was probably thirty years old. It's doubtful that many fish survive half as many years under today's intense angling pressure.

Although stocks of Atlantic coastal striped bass began to rise after World War I, the vacuum left by the defunct New England bass clubs meant the region didn't recover its primary place in the striper chronicles until after World War II. In the meantime, Baltimorean Tom Loving used a five-ounce bamboo fly rod and a quillhead streamer—which he called the Loving Feathered Minnow—to catch hundreds of stripers weighing between two and twenty-two pounds. His success was publicized by Joe Brooks, and some New Englanders assumed that if you hoped to catch a striper on a fly rod, you had to go to Maryland to do it.

Massachusetts, however, had its own prewar fly-rodding pioneer. Clarence ("Coots") Hauthaway believed that "the closer to home you fish, the more points you get." When stripers in his home waters of Plymouth Harbor were reluctant to take a single fly, he used the fly fisher's equivalent of an umbrella rig—casting as many as eight flies at a time on a fourteen-foot, two-handed Leonard rod. According to Ollie Rodman, the "problem [Coots] hadn't licked was taking stripers in fairly shallow clear water. Even when they were feeding, they ignored the best fly that Coots could cast and that is saying a lot. Finally, in desperation, he decided that the striper in clear calm water could distinguish the fly as a fake just before the strike. This led Coots to think that if he presented a 'school' of six or eight flies at once, the striper might, in his greediness, smash into them and grab fast before the 'school' escaped. And it worked!! We asked Coots if the flies didn't tangle and he said, 'Sure, but not as a rule until I've fastened into a fish.'"

Still, tangling must have been a problem, because Coots's son, Bart, couldn't recall his father ever using more than three flies at a time.

Coots (Harvard '10) and Bart (Harvard '46) were groomed for careers in chemistry and journalism, respectively, but both were too independent for preplanned lives. They pursued their bliss rather than conventional notions of success. As a result, Ollie Rodman described Coots as an "unusual combination of naturalist, ichthyologist, scientist, photographer, fly-tier, enthusiast and inquisitive fisherman. It was not enough for him to know that a certain lure took fish; he had to know why, how, when, etc. We believe that he tied more sizes, shapes and color patterns in striper lures from flies to weighted feather lures for surf casting than any man who ever lived. And he took stripers—lots of them."

Coots died in 1942 at the age of fifty-six. Yet Ollie's description of him could just as easily be applied to Bart, with the addition of the son's many contributions to the development of modern canoes and kayaks. In 1960, Bart began building a variety of small, manually powered boats, and for years he served as the unofficial coach of America's Olympic kayak team. "None of us were any good," he recalls today, "but then none were any better at the time." Bart eventually had a falling-out with the Olympic Committee, just as he'd had earlier with the Old Town Company, for whom he'd once designed canoes. About the time I bought a Hauthaway duck punt in 1975, Bart was also fighting with the Coast Guard over its determination to impose bureaucratic standards on the design of one-man boats. Bart won his argument with the Coast Guard, but lost his fights with Old Town and the Olympic Committee, not because he was wrong in the latter cases, but because he'd found a few more people in the Coast Guard who knew nearly as much about small craft as he did.

When I touched base with Bart in September 1995, he'd caught 436 striped bass on the fly so far that season. Only one of the fish, however, was above the thirty-four-inch minimum legal length in Massachusetts. Bart was unhappy about rules that neither produce more stripers nor give the angler any freedom of choice.

"Limits should concern numbers of fish, not sizes," said Bart. "We should be able to keep any size striper we like. We'd kill that one fish and quit fishing. If the state worries about us keeping too many, it should issue striper tags the way it does for deer and turkey—though, Lord knows, I dread paperwork more than most!"

# · 12 ·

# THE KENNEBEC RIVER

MARTHA'S VINEYARD MAY be New England's saltwater fly-fishing Mecca, but the Kennebec is its Eden. Dark green woods and granite outcroppings frame picturesque homes, wildflower meadows, and your own methodical casting to swirling eddies as you drift slowly with the tide toward a flock of herring gulls resting on the water—a sure sign that striped bass have recently fed in the area. Suddenly the birds are up, swooping, hovering, squabbling over splashes on both sides of the boat so you don't know which way to cast—not that it matters much, since you can't strip your fly back to the boat from any direction without getting a tug, maybe two—or, more often, the solid pull of a well-hooked fish.

Most of the stripers my son and I caught that Sunday morning in June were sixteen to twenty-one inches long, but larger fish would occasionally grab our flies and run out our seven- and eight-weight lines into their backing. Anticipation of this is what distinguishes fly fishing on the Kennebec from schoolie fishing on other tidal waters, where older fish are scarce and where, if you're catching many sixteen-inch fish, you'll hook few, if any, larger stripers. Yet each millimeter of growth over about twenty inches results in a noticeable broadening of a striper's shoulders, deepening of its belly, and increase in its capacity to resist capture. I had already caught and released a number of Kennebec fish of up to twenty-four inches when I got a strike several magnitudes greater—a fish at least thirty inches long.

Big stripers may not rush off at the break-tippet speeds of bonefish and little tunny, but in guiding my previously stripped line from the deck back onto the tackle, I remembered the electric thrill I felt as a youngster whenever I hooked a hefty fish on a handline. Brad Burns, our Kennebec host, came forward from where he'd just tagged and released another of Christopher's stripers to see how much backing I had left. I palmed the reel to increase drag pressure, but the line continued to melt away.

"Fly fishing is the most intimate way you can fish," Brad observed, "and still be a sportsman."

Brad tagged a total of thirty-six stripers that morning—about half of the number Christopher and I caught—but he didn't get to tag my big fish. Just as he slid his hand down the leader to her mouth, the striper bucked and gyrated free of the barbless hook. Brad later used a net to land, tag, and release a thirty-four-incher he caught on the eleven-weight "heavy artillery" he brought out to fish a deep ledge known as The Hump. I'd also switched to a fast-sinking line to cast a bulky nine-inch fly called Brock's Groceries, which looks more like a teaser than a lure, and which whistled weirdly and rather ominously when I whipped it past my ear on the backcast. A big fly will certainly get a big striper's attention, but a fast-sinking line is more important to regularly hooking big fish than big flies are. If your lure is on or near bottom, where the big fish feed, surprisingly small offerings will provoke them as well as a mouthful will.

When we'd started fishing that morning, Christopher had hooked fewer large fish than I did, because his Teeny seven-weight line didn't sink as fast—and, therefore, as deep before he began retrieving his fly—as my intermediate eight-weight line. Yet the two-footers that Christopher caught that day gave proportionately as good an account of themselves as the thirty-four-inch striper Brad hoisted up from The Hump. In addition, Christopher had more fun casting to fish he occasionally saw seize the fly than he would have had casting the equivalent of a coaxial cable, then waiting long seconds like a bait fisherman for the fly to reach bottom. My son's heartfelt delight, Brad's quiet satisfaction, the misty setting, and the continual action all added up to the happiest two hours of striped bass fishing of my life.

Bradford E. Burns has the strong will and prickly temperament of a self-made man who has spent much of his life bucking conventional thinking and who has, more often than not, been right. The oldest of three brothers, Brad was born on October 17, 1950, in Friendship, Maine. He grew up fishing off docks and lobster piers for mackerel, pollock, and occasional flounder. When he was ten, he caught his first schoolie stripers using blood worms trailed off a hook and drifted into eddies around bridge piers. As soon as he learned to cast plugs, he upped his average size of bass from three or four pounds to five or six.

"A seven- or eight-pounder," he recalls, "was braggable."

Brad's dad worked at the Bath Iron Works—a career path Brad decided early on he didn't want to follow. After graduating from Babson College in Boston, he went to work for a photocopying service, which he soon expanded and eventually took over, selling the company in 1995 in order to devote more time to striped bass conservation.

Years earlier, Maine biologist Lewis N. Flagg had told Brad that the Kennebec had once had a spawning population of striped bass. In the 1930s, however, that gene pool had been eradicated, partly from overfishing, but mostly due to severe pollution and eutrophication of the river. Thanks to the federal Clean Water Act, however, water quality improved in the Kennebec during the '70s. In 1977, Brad began using American Littoral Society tags to confirm what had long been assumed about the origins of the majority of Maine's migratory stripers: that a small percentage comes from the Hudson River, but most are long-distance travelers from the Chesapeake.

On October 10, 1996, one of the fish that Christopher and I had caught with Brad in June was recaptured and released in

Nauset Inlet on the elbow of Cape Cod. Although the seven-teen-incher may have subsequently turned west, entered Long Island Sound, and navigated to the Hudson via the East River, its most likely course was south to Montauk Point and down the Atlantic coast to the mouth of the Chesapeake Bay.

Atlantic coastal stocks continued to tumble in the 1970s and early '80s. At the same time, Maine's resource bureaucracy was divided equally—and ineffectually—between depart-ments of conservation, environmental protection, inland fish-eries and wildlife, and marine resources. Furthermore, no one was very keen about any species that lacked the adipose fins of trout and salmon. But Brad and a handful of like-minded an-glers—including book author John N. Cole—pushed and prodded the public agencies to try to reestablish a breeding population of Kennebec stripers. In '82 and '83, the state stocked, respectively, 190 and 200 fingerling stripers seined and transported from the Hudson. Larger stockings of several thousand fingerlings began in '84. These fish resulted from a mitigation plan for those lost on the intake screens of Consol-idated Edison's power plants on the Hudson. The hatchery at Verplanck, New York, generally grew a surplus of fingerlings to ensure that enough stripers would be available for stocking the Hudson. Since Con Ed's lawyers didn't want to see a single striper more than required by terms of the mitigation agree-ment put into the river, the hatchery people at Verplanck were happy to see the extra fish go to Maine.

Brad and John were kept informed by hatchery insiders as to how many fish might be available during a given year. One year, however, Maine officials refused to accept any Hudson River fish for fear they might be contaminated with zebra mussel larvae. Brad pointed out that keeping the fish in brackish water for a week would kill the freshwater mussels, but the biologists wouldn't budge. Unlike their nineteenth-century predecessors, who facilitated private initiative, modern government biologists (biocrats) seem more concerned with forms, procedures, and maintaining control than with achieving goals. Still, Brad and John persisted and eventually different Hudson River fish were sent; the Kennebec's striper stockings continued. Today, many local sportsmen give Brad and John the lion's share of the credit for the restoration of the fishery. Yet neither of them wants any credit. They figure the striper itself deserves all the glory.

Nor does John Cole want any credit for the pivotal role played by his 1978 book, *Striper: A Story of Fish and Man*, in restoring striped bass all along the Atlantic Coast. The book is less a conservation manifesto than the autobiography of a World War II combat veteran who exchanged the gray flannel suit of a commuter for the oilskins of a Long Island haulseiner. Just as Herman Melville used whaling to explore the consequences of obsession, Cole used beach-netting to describe the fate of free-spirited men in a world with too many people and too much technology.

As founder of the *Maine Times* and occasional contributor to the *Atlantic, New York Times, Harper's, Yankee,* and *Esquire,* Cole was able to get *Striper* widely reviewed. One of those re-

views was seen by U.S. Senator John Chafee, who picked up a
copy of the book on a weekend trip home to Rhode Island. He
read *Striper* on the plane back to Washington and, the next
morning, presided over a subcommittee hearing on the reau-
thorization of the Anadromous Fish Conservation Act. This
law concerned mostly salmon, shad, and herring. Senator
Chafee wanted to know why the striped bass wasn't getting a
larger piece of the research and restoration pie. The striper is,
after all, an anadromous species and of far greater economic
importance along the Atlantic Coast than salmon, shad, and
herring combined. The striper was also in dire decline. Quot-
ing Cole's book, Senator Chafee noted that the most recent annual Rhode Island Striper Tournament had failed to produce a
single fish, "even though hundreds of surfcasters and boat
fishermen tried for several days to land one, [and] in past
years, the same event had produced thousands of pounds."

Four men sat before the Senate subcommittee that Monday
morning. Two were mere functionaries from the National Marine Fisheries Service and the U.S. Fish and Wildlife Service,
but the other two might have been placed there by Divine
Providence. One was Irwin Alperin, executive director of the
Atlantic States Marine Fisheries Commission (ASMFC), and
an authority on striped bass. The other was John S. Gottschalk,
a former director of the U.S. Fish and Wildlife Service, a former assistant to the director of the National Marine Fisheries
Service, and, at the time of the hearing, executive director of
the International Association of Fish and Wildlife Agencies.
Gottschalk had run the U.S. Fish and Wildlife Service's re-

gional office in Boston when that agency still had a marine recreational fisheries component. He knew the economic impact of striped bass fishing in New England. The senator, Alperin, and Gottschalk soon turned the hearing into a discussion of ways that federal authority and funding could be used to save the striper. An amendment to the Anadromous Fish Conservation Act, known as the Emergency Striped Bass Act, was written that night by Gottschalk, refined the next day by subcommittee attorney Jim Range, pushed through the House of Representatives by John Breaux of Louisiana, and soon signed into law.

As it turned out, the research and stocking programs paid for with "emergency funds" were less important than the act itself, which gave the striped bass quasi-federal status. This enabled Alperin's ASMFC to develop an interstate management plan for striped bass and, in 1984, to declare its authority to shut down all manner of striped bass fishing in any state that refused to comply with the ASMFC plan. However, since a majority of participating states had to approve any such closure, it was not the ASMFC that finally started the striper on the road to recovery, but an increasingly impatient U.S. Congress, which, on October 31, 1984, approved a moratorium on all commercial netting of Atlantic striped bass.

The following spring, Maryland's secretary of the Department of Natural Resources—a nonprofessional administrator and medical doctor named Torrey Brown—persuaded Governor Harry Hughes to shut down all forms of fishing for striped bass, including intentional catch-and-release angling, in the coastal state most closely identified with the species. Since Maryland is the wellspring of a major share of Atlantic stripers, the closure of its fishery set a moral as well as a management standard for other states. In 1987, Virginia's Marine Resources Commission—renowned for its cavalier attitude toward even the most fundamental conservation measures—followed suit and shut down its own striped bass fishery.

Meanwhile, research continued to focus on every possibile cause for the striper's decline but the obvious one of overfishing. Although Cole himself had pointed out the tremendous impact of the Montauk charter fleet, which fished two and even three parties per boat per day during the height of the season, he—like most other commentators at the time—focused on pollution as the primary cause of the striper's collapse.

Anglers have always denied that the fishing we do can deplete a species. Fly fishermen feel especially superior in this regard, since many of us release most of what we catch. How can our impact possibly be compared with that of commercial netting?

The answer lies in the great and growing numbers of recreational fishermen. Even if a fly fisherman releases everything he catches, he inevitably kills a few deeply hooked or exhausted fish per season. And, of course, most sportfishermen don't release everything they catch. The National Marine Fisheries Service (NMFS) estimates that, each year, 3.2 million resident anglers, and another 1 million tourist anglers, pursue striped bass along the Atlantic Coast. Even if the average angler kills only one or two stripers per year, that mortality figure means several million adult fish—including many prime breeders—removed annually from the system.

When you factor in the number of "sportsmen" who buy cut-rate, part-time commercial licenses that entitle them to sell several hundred striped bass each season for money most don't need—as otherwise well-paid doctors, lawyers, and airline pilots—the recreational impact spirals toward the level of the estimated ten thousand full-time commercial fishermen from Maine to North Carolina.

Nonetheless, all commercial fishing for wild striped bass must stop as a precondition to quality management. Striped bass have the capacity to endure several poor years of reproduction, then rally back to optimum numbers after only one or two fortunate springs. This is because each striper can survive ten or more spawning seasons. Biologists, however, are locked into the notion that it's best to manage stripers for maximum sustained yield (MSY), meaning that most fish get to spawn only once before being caught and shipped off to market. That allows little leeway for human error or natural catastrophe. It also ensures that very few striped bass ever reach the sizes most sought by recreational fishermen. Once a majority of anglers realize that MSY management favors netters, commercial fishing will join market shooting in the annals of conservation history.

And there's no good economic reason to continue commercial fishing for wild stripers. The 1984 netting moratorium proved that striped bass aquaculture can take up the slack. Even after commercial fishing recommenced, many markets have continued to insist on the more reliable delivery schedules and standardized size of pond-reared striped bass and striper/white bass hybrids. In 1994, for example, some 8.5 million pounds of farmed stripers were sold nationwide. This total exceeded the catch of wild fish and, as John Merwin pointed out in the April 1995 issue of *Field & Stream,* it "would doubtless expand to fill market demands if commercially caught wild fish were not available."

Ending commercial fishing, however, will not end the debate over what constitutes quality angling. Too many recreational fishermen think that a trophy is always the biggest fish, especially one caught in a high-stakes tournament. A minority realize that a trophy experience hinges on such subtle factors as the tackle used, the setting, and your companions. For example, the biggest striped bass Brad Burns has yet caught on a fly was forty-six inches long. That fish, however, was caught from a boat at Fisher's Island, New York. By contrast, Brad's most *memorable* striper on a fly was thirty-six inches long, but caught from shore just below his home in Maine. And he released her—just as he does all the stripers he catches these days.

Of course, most anglers are not going to develop into catch-and-release fly fishermen. Still, Brad is disappointed that sportfishing clubs don't set higher standards for themselves. He has learned from reading old angling books that club rules a century ago were generally more demanding than those we abide by today, despite our having so many more technological advantages over the fish. For example, whereas commercial fishermen have always felt they had the option of using more than one line at a time, no 1890s sportsman would have dreamed of doing so. Most even felt that it was unethical to fight a fish sitting down—unless the angler were in a canoe—or accept assistance of any kind—unless he were handicapped, a novice, or (forgive the Victorians) an "anglerette." Moreover, if a fish was hooked any place other than the mouth, it was released as not having been "fair caught."

When charter fishing came into vogue after World War I, many skippers thought it too much to ask newcomers to the sport to hold a rod all day long and fight a fish standing up. Once, however, the use of gunwale-mounted rod holders became an acceptable way to drift baits or troll lures, it was inevitable that chartermen would begin drifting or trolling as many lines as they could to increase the odds of getting fish for their clients. It also became inevitable that chartermen would insist their clients sit down while fighting fish so the mate and skipper could turn the chair and run the boat to maximum advantage. Of course, inadvertently snagged fish went into the box alongside fair-caught ones.

In the nineteenth century, striped bass angling had been a patrician pastime, and the upper class had codes for every kind of social behavior. Anglers were kept honest by the continual exercise of conscience reinforced by peer pressure. But the old clubs died when the striped bass disappeared, and their superior angling standards died with them.

When the middle class took up marine angling following World War I, the guides—many of them former commercial fishermen—established new and more flexible standards of sportsmanship, so that even the most inexperienced or inept angler could catch a record "according to the rules." What was allowed in charter fishing gradually became the standard in most forms of fishing. Although the International Game Fish Association has tried to raise the bar a bit, the goal of most anglers continues to be to catch the largest, or the greatest accumulated poundage, of fish under the most rudimentary rules of sportsmanship. And whereas competition was once regarded as a corrosive force in angling, even conservation groups now use angling contests as a means of raising money and publicizing their cause.

If fishing one line, one lure, and one hook at a time—and then fighting a fish standing up without any assistance and releasing the quarry once it's at hand—is aesthetically so much more satisfying than the alternatives, why don't more marine angling clubs encourage such behavior, rather than always rewarding the killing of the biggest fish? And why are fly fishermen generally more conscious of angling ethics? Do the techniques of fly fishing force fly anglers to set higher standards for themselves? Or could it be that the generally greater ethical traditions of fly fishing are precisely what attract increasing numbers of people to this specialized facet of the sport?

Over the past several seasons, Brad Burns has hosted a number of fishermen as unfamiliar with fly tackle as he was himself not so many years ago. He keeps spinning and bait-casting rods on hand for their use, but in showing them how easy it is to use a fly rod, and how much fun they can have with one, he has converted several of his guests into avid fly fishermen.

He uses the same approach in striped bass conservation. Although the state of Maine feels it knows all it needs to know about the movement of stripers in and out of the Kennebec, Brad funds an ongoing tagging study of Kennebec-caught fish to sensitize politicians and resource administrators who'd not otherwise give the Kennebec or striped bass a second thought. When Brad urged the state to run the tagging program, he was told it would cost too much money and time. So Brad runs the program himself, spending less than he donates annually to local charities, plus only about five hours of paperwork per year.

When the states and federal government declared Atlantic coastal stripers fully recovered in 1990, Brad was skeptical, to say the least. He knew, as many other anglers suspected, that the real reason the states and federal government were so eager to open up sportfishing again was to reopen netting. Brad conferred with Rip Cunningham, publisher of *Salt Water Sportsman,* over ways to prevent the politicians and biocrats from completely undoing what five years of restraint had begun. The only organization in the nation that seemed to share their concerns was the Houston-based Coastal Conservation Association. Massachusetts angler Terry Tessin had been a member in Texas and knew the CCA's prime mover, Walter W. Fondren III. Phone calls led to meetings, and meetings soon led to the founding of a New England chapter. By 1992, enough of the region's marine anglers were organized to start separate chapters in Maine, Massachusetts, and Connecticut.

Conservation, like other politics, is local. The best way to recruit support for a national objective is to prove its efficacy in your own backyard. That's what Brad Burns and the Maine CCA have done with the Kennebec. The organization wanted to restore a spawning population of stripers and turn the river into an angling showcase. State officials were persuadable— less because they cared about striped bass than because they'd already written off the Kennebec as a salmon river due to the many dams that impede the upstream movement of fish. Today, the Kennebec and the connecting Sheepscot are the only rivers in the state with a closed season for striped bass. The abundance of stripers there compared with estuaries elsewhere in New England proves, once again, that quality angling hinges on catch-and-release management.

Kennebec regulations close the season to all but catch-and-release fishing from November 1 to July 1. Only single-hook artificial lures are used—although the one hook may be a treble. Since some spawning may still be in progress, the CCA wanted to extend the river's catch-and-release season to July 15. At a public hearing held to discuss the proposal, the majority of speakers endorsed the idea. State resource commissioners, however, felt their control was slipping away, so they declared the hearing "insufficiently advertised" and rejected the plan.

And so, within twenty-four hours, the river changes from a hospitable place for anglers to a highly competitive and overcrowded arena dominated by meat fishermen. Live eels are the preferred bait and, too often, letting the stripers swallow them, the preferred hooking technique. It's mediocre recreation at best, and the worst part is knowing that too few

Fourth-of-July fishermen on the river have any appreciation for striped bass.

Brad's politicking on behalf of the Kennebec has taught him two valuable lessons. First, it matters less how many people support a proposal than how many people oppose it. Elected officials and administrators may receive hundreds of letters in favor of something, but let them receive just one complaint, and they'll drop support like a hot potato.

Second, although politicians claim they'll back anglers once we collect data proving that recreationally caught and released stripers are more valuable to society than commercially landed fish, the truth is that economic arguments bore politicians. They're as locked into their idea of "fairness" as biologists are into MSY management. And just as never enough big stripers survive under MSY management to satisfy a majority of recreational fishermen, never enough stripers of any size survive to satisfy commercial interests demanding their "fair share." Yet the current concept of fairness is itself unfair, because high recreational size limits do little more than subsidize commercial exploitation.

Brad rhetorically asked in an article for the February 1994 issue of *Salt Water Sportsman,* "If the average [New England] recreational angler must return home empty-handed, why should there be an allotment of the resource for a handful of commercial fishermen to catch unlimited numbers daily?

"Logically, considering the hundreds of thousands of recreational anglers pursuing striped bass, their modest personal use should come before any commercial allotment is made.

Commercial fishermen argue that they represent the non-fishing public resource owner who chooses to consume, but not catch fish. But there are approximately fifteen people alive [in the United States] for every wild striper in the ocean. People cannot simply assign their personal allocations for someone else to consume. . . .

"Like any other business, commercial fishing is a service to the public, not a financial entitlement. Commercial fishing dates back to times of plenty when fishing for personal use was a luxury. Now we find that only modest personal consumption of these wild resources is possible. A commercial allotment no longer makes sense for a fragile inshore anadromous species like the striped bass.

"It's time to reject the old management concepts. We must recognize the far greater value that striped bass represent by existing in abundance to enhance the outdoor experiences of hundreds of thousands of urban East Coast residents and to teach them conservation and appreciation for this wild and beautiful species through catch-and-release fishing."

Brad's dream of national gamefish status for the striped bass is shared by increasing numbers of anglers, and state chapters of the Coastal Conservation Association from Maine to North Carolina are working to make that dream a reality. Ironically, however, the very abundance of striped bass today is working against that dream, because it's difficult to get political support for this proposal so long as the good times are rolling. Yet, just as surely as the lessons that might have been learned from the failures of fisheries managers in the past have been forgotten by the present generation of biologists, the Atlantic coastal striper will once again decline. Then, perhaps—in its darkest hour—the striped bass will be granted gamefish status, and the more important debate over angling ethics can finally begin.

# · *Appendix I* ·

# STRIPED BASS AGE, LENGTH, AND WEIGHT RELATIONSHIPS

STRIPER SIZES VARY according to sex, season, and availability of food. From their third year on, females grow faster and generally larger than males. In a Maryland study, 91.2 percent of all fish of over fifteen pounds were females. Large males do exist, however. In the spring of 1958, a forty-pound, forty-five-plus-inch male was caught in Maryland's Nanticoke River. However, almost all older fish (seventeen or more years) are females. By that age, lengths and weights are closely correlated. For example, a fifty-inch striper weighs about fifty pounds and is at least eighteen years old. The oldest recorded striper was a thirty-one-year-old fish from the Chesapeake.

# THE STRIPED BASS CHRONICLES

---

| Age in Years | Average Length (in inches) | Average Weight (in pounds and ounces) |
|:---:|:---:|:---:|
| 1 | 4.0–5.5 | 0/2–0/4 |
| 2 | 9.8–12.0 | 0/11–1/1 |
| 3 | 13.4–15.4 | 1/10–2/1 |
| 4 | 17.0–18.5 | 2/8–3/10 |
| 5 | 19.7–21.9 | 3/9–6/7 |
| 6 | 22.0–26.4 | 6/3–9/15 |
| 7 | 24.0–29.5 | 9/3–14/3 |
| 8 | 29.0–32.0 | 12/5–18 |
| 9 | 32.7–34.5 | 17/3–23/15 |
| 10 | 34.5–36.4 | 20/8–28/2 |
| 11 | 35.7–37.5 | 24/3–31/4 |
| 12 | 39.0–40.7 | 27/9–37/8 |
| 13 | 40.0–41.0 | 31/5–41/4 |
| 14 | 41.3–42.5 | 35/1–49/6 |
| 15 | 43.0 | 38/5 |
| 16 | 44.0 | 41/9 |

# · *Appendix II* ·

# TWENTY YEARS AGO

Just as adult attitudes are shaped by youthful experiences, nations are their history. Yet one of America's most consistent themes is our rejection of history and the lessons we might learn from it. "So we beat on," F. Scott Fitzgerald observed, "boats against the current, borne back ceaselessly into the past."

On February 17, 1976, the International Game Fish Association, National Coalition for Marine Conservation, National Marine Fisheries Service, National Oceanic and Atmospheric Administration, and Sport Fishing Institute cooperatively sponsored what many participants hoped would become an annual series of marine recreational fishing symposiums. I was asked to anchor the closing panel chaired by Hal Lyman, then owner of *Salt Water Sportsman* magazine. This is how I began:

"Saltwater anglers are nothing if not confused these days. Arguments over recreational fishing licenses; the morality, if not legality, of certain angling accessories and lures; and whether the federal government should have ultimate responsibility for the entire mess swirl about us even as we wade into the surf for another cast.

"If you think I exaggerate, let's take an odyssey through the rules and regulations governing a single marine species: the striped bass. In honor of our southern hosts [the symposium was held in New Orleans], let's start with the sovereign states of Georgia, South Carolina, and North Carolina. The first two categorize the striped bass (or 'rockfish,' as the species is called in the regulations) as a gamefish and, therefore, prohibit its sale or capture with nets. North Carolina, however, has a major net fishery for stripers whose only restrictions are that the minimum mesh size be 2½ inches and that the owner of a commercial fishing vessel pay for his license at the rate of 50 cents per vessel-foot.

"Thus, some young striped bass produced in the rivers of Georgia and South Carolina, and protected as gamefish in those two states, run an excellent chance of winding up in mid-Atlantic restaurants if they follow their migratory urge and wander across state lines into North Carolina. Furthermore, whereas South Carolina restricts her sportsmen to ten striped bass a day, North Carolina has no limits whatsoever.

"Are these contrasting, possibly conflicting, rules based on scientific knowledge and judgment? Have such restrictions and nonrestrictions been established for the optimum sustainable yield of the species, taking into account the interests of both commercial and sportfishermen?

"Of course not. North Carolina, being less distant from major metropolitan markets than other southern coastal states, long ago established a late-winter/early-spring fishery for striped bass—when these fish were otherwise unavailable to consumers in Philadelphia, New York, and Boston. Outer Bankers were able to kill striped bass—along with ducks, geese, and swans—for Yankee buyers and stand a reasonable chance, in cool weather, of having the fish and game arrive without spoiling. Market hunting began winding down in 1913 with passage of the Weeks-McLean Act that gives responsibility for migratory bird management to the federal government, but sixty-three [now eighty-four] years after that, market fishermen and local politicians still dictate management policies for the striped bass, which is no less a migratory species than the black duck.

"For other examples of administrative confusion, let's cross the continent to California and Oregon, the two Pacific states that sustain saltwater populations of stripers, some of which wander up and down the coast—since that's how Oregon got its striped bass populations in the first place. Yet the sportfishing limit for Oregon is five stripers a day; for California, it's three. Where's the logic?[1]

---

[1]The current sportfishing limits are two fish per day in both states, but California's minimum size is eighteen inches, while Oregon's is thirty inches. Again, where's the logic?

"Furthermore, although both states have declared the striped bass to be a gamefish and, therefore, illegal to net, until recently an escape clause in the Oregon law permitted shad netters to sell their 'incidental catch' of stripers, which normally exceeds fifty-four thousand pounds a year.[2] These bass were allegedly donated to charitable institutions. But whatever their use, fifty-four thousand pounds are a lot of fish. Are there really so many Oregon stripers that stocks can sustain such a significant by-catch—remember, only reported fish are donated to charity; how many unreported stripers are sold?—plus five fish a day to anglers? I doubt it. Rather, I think Oregon's generous limit is based on the hope of encouraging people to buy fishing licenses and stay at local resorts rather than on any credible assessment of what Oregon stripers can sustain in the way of angling pressure.

"In New England, the situation borders on chaos. Maine and New Hampshire both regard the striped bass as a game-fish, and no commercial netting is allowed. However, neither state has a daily angler limit, although Maine periodically calls a halt to striped bass fishing in one or another of her twelve estuaries—random rule changes some anglers regard as a calculated way for the state to raise revenue through fines, since even local fishermen run the risk of unwittingly break-

[2]Today, the combined weight of all the adult striped bass in Oregon may not be fifty-four thousand pounds.

ing the law if they're not up to date on the latest bureaucratic bulletins.[3]

"In neighboring Massachusetts, the striped bass is *neither* a commercial fish *nor* a gamefish. But, whereas striped bass can be caught by trollers, trotliners, and fish trappers, it's considered unethical to take this species with a net. On the other hand, it's considered entirely ethical for Massachusetts 'sportsmen' to sell their catch (rather than release extra fish) through the instrument of a graduated commercial license costing from $5[4] to $100. The cheaper fee is tailored for the rod-and-reeler who hopes to make a profit from his recreation, since it allows him to sell up to one hundred pounds of fish, plus one fish, per day.

"With the wholesale price of striped bass at an all-time high, a commercial angling license—talk about an oxymoron!—is a shrewd investment. True, the fish that anglers sell could have provided recreation for fishermen elsewhere if only Massachusetts anglers were encouraged to tag[5] and re-

[3]Maine now has the most restrictive striped bass limit in New England—although anglers there and elsewhere would be better off with a slot limit, rather than a thirty-six-inch minimum size. A coastwide slot that opened at, say, twenty-two inches would enable southern fishermen to keep a few of the smaller fish that predominate in the Chesapeake region; one that closed at thirty-four inches would protect capital breeders during their most fecund years.

[4]The basic cost is now $45. Considering what this permit does to undermine angling ethics and harvest management, it's a travesty, regardless of price.

[5]The American Littoral Society, Sandy Hook, Highlands, NJ 07732 (908-291-0055) has administered an amateur fish-tagging program since 1965. Volunteers tag and release approximately twelve thousand striped bass annually, with an average reported recovery rate of 4 percent. The actual recovery rate is undoubtedly higher, but since most commercial fishermen return tags only when a significant cash reward is offered, we'll never know how much higher. What we do know, however, provides some fascinating stories. For example, beginning in 1989 and ending in 1993 (her last known capture and release), the same striped bass was taken at least once a year in either Connecticut or New York State. When last reported, the fish was nearly forty inches long and weighed over thirty pounds. Who says we can't stockpile prime breeders through catch-and-release fishing?

lease their extra stripers. But no. In the present realm of marine management, it's every state and fisherman for himself.

"The examples of confusion in the regulation of this single species continue down the coast. Rhode Island designates the striped bass as both a gamefish *and* a commercial fish. In neighboring Connecticut, it's a gamefish only, and some anglers are presently attempting to pass a law requiring a sportfishing license to fish the state's tidal rivers where striped bass occur.[6]

"New York and New Jersey have some confusing size and possession limits. New Jersey requires that a kept fish be eighteen inches or longer; in New York, sixteen inches will suffice. However, New Jersey measures fish from the snout to the tip of the tail, whereas New York measures from the snout to the fork of the tail. That we're unable to standardize even the way fish are measured in neighboring states is suggestive of how difficult it will be to persuade jurisdictions to agree on anything more substantive.[7]

"New Jersey permits commercial fishermen to keep striped bass that are six to eight inches shorter (depending on the type of gear used) than the stripers that recreational anglers are al-

---

[6]This effort failed, and from Maine to North Carolina, it's still possible to fish for migratory stripers without a license. Although Maryland and Virginia require a license to fish the Chesapeake, no license is required to fish in either state's Atlantic coastal waters.

[7]New York and New Jersey finally agreed on a snout-to-tip-of-tail standard for measuring fish, but that's about all they've agreed on. For instance, you have to be careful about where in the Hudson River you catch fish. On the New York side, the daily limit is one striper at least eighteen inches long; on the New Jersey side, it's two stripers a day at least twenty-eight inches long.

lowed to keep. Furthermore, although it's illegal to net striped bass within three miles of the Jersey coast in the Atlantic, stripers can be taken with a net in the Jersey portion of Delaware Bay.[8]

"In Delaware, netting is legal, but only between November 2 and August 30. Furthermore, beach seines and drifting gill nets are legal, while pound nets and trawls are not. Delaware also stipulates that no striped bass shall be kept of *less* than twelve inches or *more* than twenty pounds—requiring anglers to carry both a ruler and a scale![9]

"Delaware also permits the use of spears and spearguns to take striped bass, but New Jersey doesn't. At least, New Jersey *says* it prohibits spear fishing for stripers. A subclause in the regulations exempts divers who 'goggle fish' in the waters of the Atlantic. Goggle fishing is then defined as 'taking fish by means of a spear, harpoon, dart, arrow, or other missile, hand held and hand propelled by the fisherman while he is completely submerged in the water.' I'm glad the regs clarified that; for a moment I thought New Jersey allowed spear fishing for striped bass![10]

"In Maryland and Virginia, the two states sharing the mother lode of the Chesapeake, administrators seem constitu-

---

[8]New Jersey finally eliminated this discrepancy when it made the striped bass a gamefish in 1991.

[9]Delaware has simplified the matter to a twenty-eight-inch minimum, but abandoned the superior slot limit in the process.

[10]Despite gamefish status, New Jersey still allows "goggle fishing" for striped bass. The limit is two speared fish per day.

tionally unable to agree on a common management plan for striped bass or even to discard old rules contradicted by new ones. As a result, anglers in each state are warned that the fishing regulations are 'quite complicated,' and the Virginia Marine Resources Commission urges Commonwealth anglers to purchase a book covering all tidal laws. Is this something bureaucrats really expect ordinary fishermen to do?

"I'm sure that administrative justifications can be found for each and every one of the rules I've cited. I'm equally sure, however, that . . . nowhere in the wording of any state's laws is there the least acknowledgment that the striped bass is a migratory species shared by a majority of Atlantic coastal states as well as the Maritime Provinces in Canada.

"So herein lies my point: If the states will not confer to manage a resource common to all, the federal government has a moral obligation to step in and establish the guidelines."

Twice in 1976, I testified before Congress on behalf of an exclusive economic zone for U.S. offshore waters. Like other marine conservationists of the time, I believed that, by extending America's regulatory boundaries to two hundred miles—as most other coastal nations had already done—we could stop the plundering of our continental shelf by foreign fishing fleets. Well, we did. But we ended up with something far worse: the *regulated* plundering of our continental shelf by *domestic* fishing fleets.

As a result, the mood of the country today is very different than it was in our nation's bicentennial year. Any suggestion that the federal government has an indispensable role to play in migratory fish management is countered with examples of failed federal fisheries policies dealing with species from cod to sharks, and not excluding the striped bass. But the fact remains: There is no alternative to federal authority if we want relief from the regulatory parochialism of the states.

# · Appendix III ·

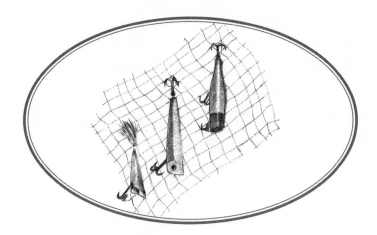

# SAVING THE PAST

O LD CLUB PUBLICATIONS are great grist for the mills of angling historians. For example, in the 1920 yearbook of the Asbury Park Fishing Club, Robert A. Inch described how three men— Cyrus Detre, Charles Showaker, and William Moynan—introduced rods and reels to northern New Jersey surf fishing. This was in about 1889, recalled Inch, who also remembered "that Detre always used Edw. vom Hofe rods and reels, while Moynan made his own rods and used Julius vom Hofe reels. As I look back, it seems to me that Moynan was one of the most expert anglers I have seen. Always neatly clad in white duck overalls, the white flaps covering his breast, a blue flannel shirt and white helmet with a rod which, accustomed as we are to John Seger's work, it would be considered even now a pleasure to fish with, and with a quiet, polished, rapidly-running reel, he presented an attractive picture."

That same yearbook included a photograph of Miss Elizabeth M. Gallaher in the act of making a record cast of 234 feet, 9 inches; a Van Campen Heilner article, "Wake Up—New Jersey!," that documented the dire consequences of unregulated menhaden fishing; a report on an expedition to the "wild" barrier islands of southern New Jersey; and many ads, including those of two notable outdoor magazines competing for the same subscribers. *Forest and Stream* called itself "A Gentleman's Magazine" and politely asked: "Your father read *Forest and Stream.* You will, some day. Why not now?" By contrast, *Field and Stream* (without an ampersand) pointed out that the only way anyone could get a contest blank for "$3,000 Worth of Prizes for the Biggest Fish" was to buy a copy of the magazine. That gimmicky approach was apparently the more effective. Within a decade, an ampersanded *Field & Stream* had absorbed what was left of *Forest and Stream.*

Marine anglers have been forming clubs and publishing newsletters for over a century. If you find a stash of antique yearbooks, catalogs, or photographs, why not donate them to the International Game Fish Association, 1301 East Atlantic Boulevard, Pompano Beach, FL 33060? For more information, call 305-941-3474; or fax 305-941-5868.

# · *Appendix IV* ·

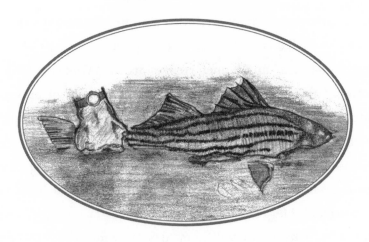

# IF YOU'D LIKE TO HELP

FOUNDED IN 1977, the Coastal Conservation Association, Inc., has over forty thousand members dedicated to perpetuating quality angling. The priority of state chapters from Maine to North Carolina is to end the sale of wild striped bass and to manage the species for optimum sustained yield. For further information and the address of your nearest chapter, write CCA, 4801 Woodway, Suite 220 West, Houston, TX 77056; or call 713-626-4222.

# List of Species

albacore, false (little tunny)—*Euthynnus alletteratus*

alewife (river herring)—*Alosa pseudoharengus*

anchovy, bay—*Anchoa mitchilli*

anchovy, Pacific (northern anchovy)—*Engraulis mordax*

bass, black—*Micropterus* spp.

bass, channel (red drum)—*Sciaenops ocellatus*

bass, common sea—*Centropristes striatus*

bass, European—*Dicentrarchus labrax*

bass, striped—*Morone saxatilis*

black duck, American—*Anas rubripes*

blood worm—*Glycera* spp.

bluefish—*Pomatomus saltatrix*

bonito, Atlantic—*Sarda sarda*

buzzard—*Buteo buteo*

cabezone—*Scorpaenichthys marmoratus*

carp, common—*Cyprinus carpio*

catfish, channel—*Ictalurus punctatus*

catfish, sea—*Galeichthys felis*

clam, soft-shelled (manoe)—*Mya arenaria*

cod, Atlantic—*Gadus morhua*

crab, blue—*Callinectes sapidus*

crab, calico (lady crab)—*Ovalipes ocellatus*

crab, sand (mole crab)—*Emerita talpoida*

crappie—*Pomoxis* spp.

dogfish, smooth—*Mustelus canis*

eagle, bald—*Haliaeetus leucocephalus*

flounder (fluke)—*Paralichthys dentatus*

halibut, California—*Paralichthys californicus*

herring, Pacific—*Clupea harengus pallasii*

herring, sea (Atlantic herring)—*Clupea harengus harengus*

ibis, scarlet—*Endocimus ruber*

kingfish, northern (king whiting or sand mullet)—
    *Menticirrhus saxatilis*

mackerel, Atlantic—*Scomber scombrus*

menhaden (mossbunker or pogy)—*Brevoortia tyrannus*

mussel, zebra—*Dreissena polymorpha*

osprey—*Pandion haliaetus*

perch, surf (surfperch)—Family Embiotocidae

perch, yellow—*Perca flavescens*

pollock—*Pollachius virens*

porgy, northern (scup)—*Stenotomus chrysops*

salmon, Atlantic—*Salmo salar*

salmon, chinook—*Oncorhynchus tshawytscha*

salmon, coho—*Oncorhynchus kisutch*

seatrout, spotted—*Cynoscion nebulosus*

shad, American—*Alosa sapidissima*

silversides, Atlantic—*Menidia menidia*

skate—*Raja* spp.

smelt, Delta—*Hypomesus transpacificus*

squid, long-finned—*Loligo pealei*

sucker—*Catostomus* spp.

swordfish—*Xiphias gladius*

tautog—*Tautoga onitis*

vulture, turkey—*Cathartes aura*

weakfish (squeteague or gray seatrout)—*Cynoscion regalis*

whelk—*Busycon* spp.

# BIBLIOGRAPHY

Abrames, J. Kenney. *Striper Moon*. Portland, Ore.: Frank Amato Publications, 1994.

Adams, Leon David. *Striped Bass Fishing in California and Oregon*. Palo Alto, Calif.: Pacific Books, 1953.

American Fisheries Society. *A List of Common and Scientific Names of Fishes from the United States and Canada* (third edition), Bethesda, Md., 1976.

Bickerdyke, John. *Sea Fishing*. The Badminton Library. London: Longmans, Green, and Co., 1895.

Brooks, Joe. *Salt Water Fly Fishing*. New York: G. P. Putnam's Sons, 1950.

Brooks, Win. *The Shining Tides*. New York: William Morrow and Company, 1952.

Brown, John J. *The American Angler's Guide; or, Complete Fisher's Manual, for the United States*. New York: H. Long & Brother, 1845.

Burnley, Eric B. *Surf Fishing the Atlantic Coast*. Harrisburg, Penn.: Stackpole Books, 1989.

Chatham, Russell. *Angler's Coast*. Garden City, N.Y.: Doubleday & Company, 1976.

————. "Midnight Stripers." *Field & Stream*, March 1977, pages 136–143.

————. *Striped Bass on the Fly: A Guide to California Waters*. San Francisco: Examiner Special Projects, 1977.

Cole, John N. *Fishing Came First: A Memoir*. New York: Lyons & Burford, Publishers, 1989.

———. *Striper: A Story of Fish and Man.* Boston: Little, Brown and Company, 1978.

Earnhardt, Tom. *Fly Fishing the Tidewaters.* New York: Lyons & Burford, Publishers, 1995.

Elliott, William. *Carolina Sports, by Land and Water.* Charleston, S.C.: Burges and James, 1846.

Evanoff, Vlad. *Surf Fishing.* New York: Harper & Row, 1974.

Feinberg, William M. "Asbury Park Fishing Club, or How to Stay Young at 92." *New Jersey Outdoors,* May/June 1981, pages 8–9.

———. "Northeast Striper Fishing: How Good Were the Good Old Days?" *Mid-Atlantic Game & Fish,* April 1993, pages 33–35.

Fitzgerald, F. Scott. *Three Novels of F. Scott Fitzgerald* [including *The Great Gatsby*]. New York: Charles Scribner's Sons, 1953.

Floyd-Jones, Thos. *Backward Glances, Reminiscences of an Old New-Yorker.* New York: privately printed, 1914.

Gabrielson, Ira N., ed. *The Fisherman's Encyclopedia.* Harrisburg, Penn.: Stackpole & Heck, 1950.

Gosner, Kenneth L. *A Field Guide to the Atlantic Seashore.* Boston: Houghton Mifflin Co., 1979.

Heilner, Van Campen. *Salt Water Fishing.* 1937. New York: Alfred A. Knopf, 1953.

———, and Frank Stick. *The Call of the Surf.* Garden City, N.Y.: Doubleday, Page & Co., 1920.

Herbert, Henry William. *Frank Forester's Fish and Fishing of the United States, and British Provinces of North America.* London: Richard Bentley, 1849.

Hightower, Joseph E. "Stay Tuned for Stripers." *Wildlife in North Carolina,* April 1995, pages 20–23.

# Bibliography

Hogan, Austin S. "The Historic Striped Bass: A Brief Introduction," *The American Fly Fisher,* Summer 1975, pages 7–9.

Horseman, Larry O., and Ronnie J. Kernehan. *An Indexed Bibliography of the Striped Bass,* Morone saxatilis, *1670–1976.* Middletown, Del.: Ichthyological Associates, Inc., 1976.

Hulit, Leonard. *The Salt Water Angler.* New York: D. Appleton and Company, 1924.

Karas, Nick. *The Striped Bass.* New York: Lyons & Burford, Publishers, 1993.

Lyman, Henry, and Frank Woolner. *The Complete Book of Striped Bass Fishing.* New York: A. S. Barnes and Company, 1954.

McClane, A. J., ed. *McClane's New Standard Fishing Encyclopedia and International Angling Guide.* New York: Holt, Rinehart and Winston, 1974.

McDonald, John D., ed. *The Complete Fly Fisherman: The Notes and Letters of Theodore Gordon.* New York: Charles Scribner's Sons, 1947.

Merriman, Daniel. "Notes on the Life History of the Striped Bass (*Roccus lineatus*)." *Copeia,* no. 1, April 10, 1937, n.p.

———. "Studies on the Striped Bass (*Roccus saxatilis*) of the Atlantic Coast." *Fishery Bulletin of the Fish and Wildlife Service* 35, vol. 50. Washington, D.C.: U.S. Government Printing Office, 1941.

Merwin, John. "State of the Striped Bass." *Field & Stream,* April 1995, pages 60–68.

Moss, Frank T. *Successful Striped Bass Fishing.* Camden, Maine: International Marine Publishing Co., 1974.

Muus, Bent J., and Preben Dahlstrom. *Collins Guide to the Sea Fishes of Britain and North-Western Europe.* London: Wm. Collins Sons and Co. Ltd., 1974.

Nelson, Kent. "Rockfish on the Rebound." *Wildlife in North Carolina,* March 1994, pages 8–13.

Norris, Thaddeus. *The American Angler's Book: Embracing the Natural History of Sporting Fish, and the Art of Taking Them.* Philadelphia: Porter & Coates, 1864.

Raney, Edward C., Ernest F. Tresselt, Edgar H. Hollis, V. D. Vladykov, and D. H. Wallace. *The Striped Bass* (Roccus saxatilis). New Haven, Conn.: Peabody Museum of Natural History, Yale University, December 1952.

Reiger, George. *Zane Grey, Outdoorsman.* Harrisburg, Penn.: Stackpole Books, 1992.

———. "Capitol Stripers." *Fishing World,* March/April 1969, pages 30–34.

———. "Fall for Dixie Stripers." *Field & Stream,* November 1972, pages 66–67, 166–169.

———. "Old Virginny's New Stripers." *Fishing World,* November/December 1969, pages 38–43.

———. *Profiles in Saltwater Angling.* Englewood Cliffs, N.J.: Prentice-Hall, Inc., 1973.

———. "The Role of Nongovernmental Organizations in Marine Recreational Fisheries." *Marine Recreational Fisheries,* Sport Fishing Institute, Washington, D.C., 1976.

———. "San Francisco Striped Bass Eat Flies, Plugs, Tin Squids and Anchovies—and Anchovies?" *Fishing World,* May/June 1970, pages 46–49, 58–59.

———. "The Stripers of Alcatraz." *Fishing World,* July/August 1968, pages 28–29, 58–59.

———. *Wanderer on My Native Shore.* New York: Lyons & Burford, Publishers, 1991.

# Bibliography

———. "Why the Private Management Institutions Are Not Doing More." *Marine Recreational Fisheries* 8, Sport Fishing Institute, Washington, D.C., 1983.

Robins, C. Richard, and G. Carleton Ray. *A Field Guide to Atlantic Coast Fishes North America.* Boston: Houghton Mifflin Co., 1986.

Rodman, O. H. P. *The Saltwater Fisherman's Favorite Four.* New York: William Morrow & Co., 1948.

———. *Striped Bass—Where, When and How to Catch Them.* New York: A. S. Barnes and Company, 1944.

Roosevelt, Robert Barnwell. *Game Fish of the Northern States of America and British Provinces.* New York: Carleton, 1862. (Published under the name Robert Barnwell.)

———. *Superior Fishing; Or the Striped Bass, Trout, Black Bass, and Blue-Fish of the Northern States.* New York: Orange Judd Company, 1884.

Rosko, Milt. *Secrets of Striped Bass Fishing.* New York: The Macmillan Co., 1966.

Rulifson, Roger A., and Michael J. Dadswell. "Life History and Population Characteristics of Striped Bass in Atlantic Canada." *Transactions of the American Fisheries Society* 124: 477–507, Bethesda, Md., 1995.

Scott, Genio C. *Fishing in American Waters.* New York: Harper & Brothers, 1869.

Smith, Jerome V. C. *Natural History of the Fishes of Massachusetts, Embracing a Practical Essay on Angling.* 1833. Rockville Centre, N.Y.: Freshet Press, Inc., 1970.

Spangler, A. M. *"Near By" Fresh and Salt Water Fishing, or Angling Within a Radius of One Hundred Miles of Philadelphia.* Philadelphia: Spangler & Davis, 1889.

Tabory, Lou. *Inshore Fly Fishing*. New York: Lyons & Burford, Publishers, 1992.

Twain, Mark. *Life on the Mississippi*. New York: H. O. Houghton & Company, 1874.

Walters, Keith. *Chesapeake Stripers*. Bozman, Md.: Aerie House Division, 1990.

White, Ellington. "Striped Bass and Southern Solitude." *Fisherman's Bounty*, ed. Nick Lyons. New York: Crown Publishers, Inc., 1970.

Wildwood, Will. "Memoirs of Eminent Sportsmen: Genio C. Scott." *The American Fly Fisher*, Fall 1985, pages 23–24.

Woolner, Frank, and Henry Lyman. *Striped Bass Fishing*. New York: Nick Lyons Books, 1983.

Wyckoff, William C. "The Net Result: The Work of the United States Fish Commission." *Harper's New Monthly Magazine*, vol. XLIX, June to November 1874, pages 213–229.

# INDEX